New Readers Press

W9-CAJ-272

Citizenship
Passing the Test

Second Edition

Lynne Weintraub

Citizenship: Passing the Test 2nd ed.
ISBN 1-56420-281-X
Copyright © 2002
New Readers Press
Division of ProLiteracy Worldwide
1320 Jamesville Ave., Syracuse, New York 13210

Printed in the United States of America
9 8 7 6 5

Developmental Editor: Paula Schlusberg
Copy Editor: Judi Lauber
Production Director: Heather Witt
Designer: Kimbrly Koennecke
Cover Designer: Kimbrly Koennecke
Illustrator: Linda Tiff
Production Specialist: Alexander R. Jones

All proceeds from the sale of New Readers Press materials support literacy programs
in the United States and worldwide.

Contents

1. Welcome to the United States

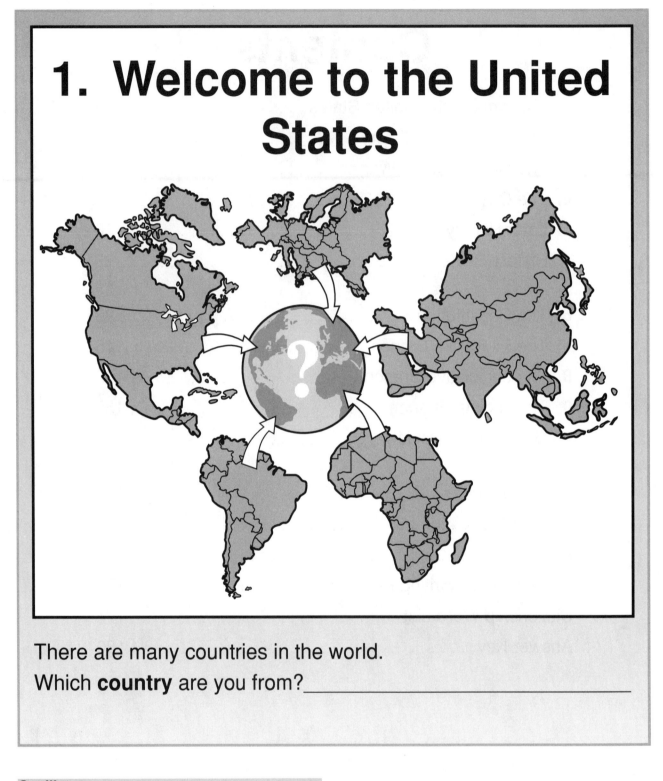

There are many countries in the world.

Which **country** are you from?_____

Spelling

you   _you_____

from   _____

Every country has a **flag.**

Can you find your home country's flag?

Spelling

flag _____

find _____

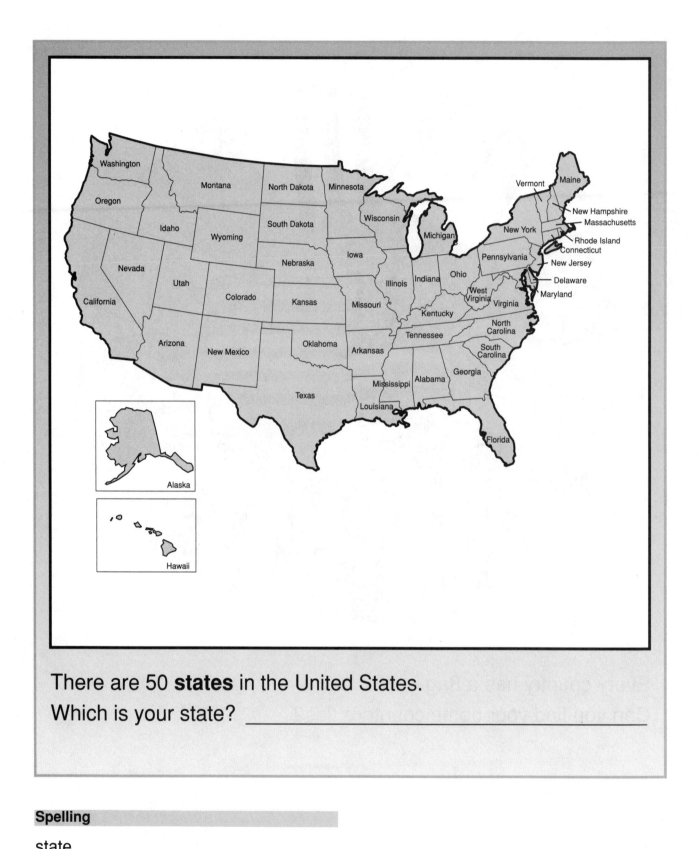

There are 50 **states** in the United States.
Which is your state? _____

Spelling

state _____

your _____

There are 50 **stars** on the U.S. flag.
The 50 stars **stand for** the 50 U.S. states.

Spelling

stars _____

What Does It Mean?

U.S. = United States

star = ★

stand for = mean

Blue

Red

White

The **colors** of the flag are red, white, and blue.
The stars are white. The **stripes** are red and white.

Spelling

red _____

white _____

blue _____

colors _____

What Does It Mean?

stripes =

Every country has an **official** song.

That song is the country's **national anthem.**

The national anthem of the U.S. is **"The Star-Spangled Banner."**

What Does It Mean?

national = of our country

anthem = song

banner = flag

An American wrote "The Star-Spangled Banner."
His name was **Francis Scott Key.**

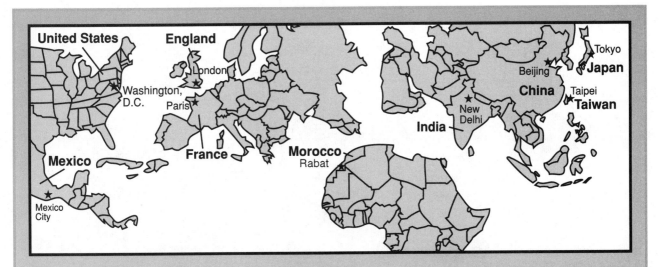

Every country has a **government.**

A country's government is in its **capital.**

The capital of the U.S. is **Washington, D.C.**

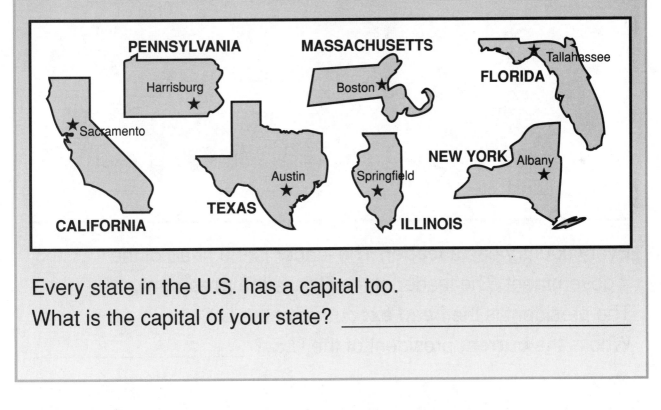

Every state in the U.S. has a capital too.

What is the capital of your state? _____

Spelling

capital _____

What Does It Mean?

government = people who are in charge

capital = city where the government is

Every country has a **leader.** The leader is the head of the government. The leader of the U.S. is the **president.**
The president is the **head executive** of the U.S.
Who is the **current** president of the U.S.? _____

The leader of a U.S. state is a **governor.**

A governor is the head executive of a U.S. state.

Who is the governor of your state? _____

The leader of a U.S. city is a **mayor.**

A mayor is the head executive of a U.S. city.

Who is the leader of your city or town? _____

Spelling

city _____

What Does It Mean?

city =

Every country has a **form of government.**

The U.S. form of government is a **democracy.**

In a democracy, people choose their own leaders.

In the U.S., we choose our leaders by voting in **elections.**

Spelling	What Does It Mean?
elections _____	form = kind
every _____	choose = pick
our _____	

There are two **major political groups** in the U.S.
One is the **Democratic Party.**
The other is the **Republican Party.**

Spelling

there _____

one _____

What Does It Mean?

major = main = important

party = political group

To vote in the U.S., a person must be old enough.
The **minimum voting age** is 18.
Citizens who are at least 18 can vote.

Spelling

old _____

What Does It Mean?

minimum = youngest

The **Statue of Liberty** stands for freedom in the U.S.
The Statue of Liberty is in New York harbor.

Spelling

freedom _____

What Does It Mean?

liberty = freedom

Match

Find the words that go with the pictures.
Copy the words on the lines.

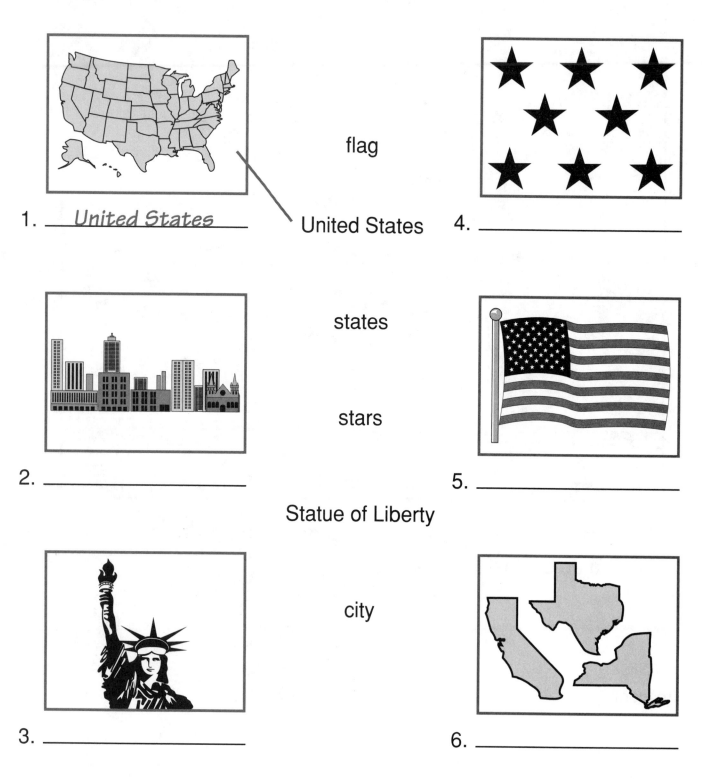

flag

United States

1. _United States_

4. _____

states

stars

2. _____

5. _____

Statue of Liberty

city

3. _____

6. _____

What Does It Mean?

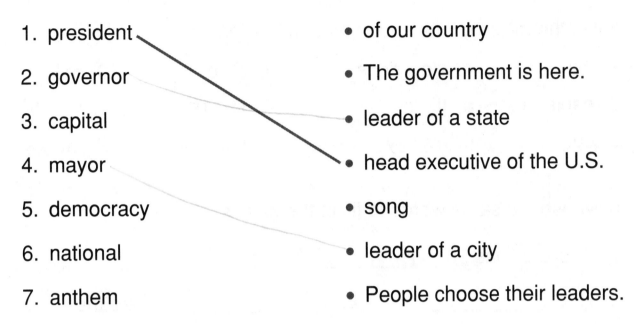

1. president — head executive of the U.S.
2. governor · leader of a state
3. capital · The government is here.
4. mayor · leader of a city
5. democracy · People choose their leaders.
6. national · of our country
7. anthem · song

Yes or No?

yes	(no)	1.	The U.S. has 52 states.
(yes)	no	2.	There are 50 stars on the flag.
yes	(no)	3.	The colors of the flag are red, white, and yellow.
yes	(no)	4.	The Statue of Liberty is in Washington, D.C.
(yes)	no	5.	The capital of the U.S. is Washington, D.C.
(yes)	no	6.	The leader of the U.S. is the president.
(yes)	no	7.	Francis Scott Key wrote "The Star-Spangled Banner."
yes	no	8.	The head executive of a state is a president.
yes	no	9.	The leader of a city is a mayor.
yes	no	10.	The government of the U.S. is a democracy.
yes	no	11.	The U.S. has one major political group.
yes	no	12.	The stars on the flag are white.

Spelling

A. Fill in the missing letters for words in this lesson.

1. blu_e_
2. capit__l
3. col__rs

4. ele__tions
5. fl__g
6. ev__ry

7. r__d
8. st__rs
9. sta__es

10. the__e
11. w__ite
12. cit__

B. Now use the same words to fill in the blanks.

1. The U.S. has 50 _states_____.

2. Red, _____ , and _____ are the colors of the flag.

3. We choose leaders by voting in _____.

4. There are 50 _____ on the U.S. flag.

5. Washington, D.C., is the _____ of the U.S.

Say the Answer

1. Who is the head of your city or town?
2. Who is the current governor of your state?
3. What is the capital of your state?
4. Who is the president of the U.S. today?
5. Who wrote "The Star-Spangled Banner"?
6. What colors are the stripes on the U.S. flag?
7. What are the colors of our flag?
8. What color are the stars on our flag?

Writing Cards—Directions

Study the Words

Read each sentence.

Copy each sentence two times on the lines.

Try to remember the letters in each word.

You will hear these sentences on the test in this lesson.

Make Writing Cards

Make Writing Cards to help you practice these sentences.

There are two ways to make the cards.

1. Make a copy of page 23 on a copy machine. Use strong paper! Use scissors to cut on the lines.

   OR

2. Get index cards. Copy each sentence three times on one index card.

Practice Listening and Writing

After you make your Writing Cards, give them to a helper.

Ask your helper to read the directions on page 22.

You will hear each sentence three times.

Write the words that you hear on a paper.

When you're finished, use the Writing Cards to check your paper.

If you see a mistake, copy the Writing Card three times to help you remember.

Then get a new paper and ask your helper to read the card to you again.

When You Take the Writing Test

Each test in this book has a writing test. You will be able to practice writing sentences that you hear.

You can play the audio recording to hear the sentences. You will hear each sentence three times. Write what you hear.

Or give your Writing Cards to a helper. Ask the helper to read each sentence to you three times. Write what you hear.

Writing Cards—Instructions for Helpers

The sentences in the Writing Cards sets in each lesson are for practicing the writing (dictation) part of the U.S. citizenship test. Sentences like the ones in the Writing Cards sets will be used in the test.

Read each sentence slowly and clearly, three (3) times, while the learner writes it.

When you have finished reading all the cards in the set, help the learner check the sentences. If there is a mistake in a sentence, the learner will copy the sentence three times. Then read that card to the learner again, three (3) times, while the learner writes the sentence again.

Writing Cards Set 1

1. The stars on the flag are white.

   The stars on the flag are white.

   _____

2. The U.S. flag has 50 stars.

   _____

   _____

3. The colors of the flag are red, white, and blue.

   _____

   _____

4. There are 50 states in the U.S.

   _____

   _____

5. The capital of the U.S. is Washington, D.C.

   _____

   _____

Test Hint #1

The examiner will ask you to write a sentence. You do not need to write perfectly. If you get most of the sentence right, you will probably pass.

What will you do if you can't spell a word? Don't give up. Try to write some of the letters in the word. Finish the sentence anyway. The examiner will see that you can write some words.

What if you don't understand a sentence?
Ask the examiner to say it again.
Or ask the examiner to explain what the sentence means.

If you still can't write the sentence, the examiner will probably give you another sentence to write.

If you can write at least one sentence right, you will probably pass.

Try the Test

Mark the answer box with the best answer for each question.

1. How many stars are on the U.S. flag?
   A. 10 stars
   B. 50 stars
   C. 52 stars
   D. 100 stars

2. Where is the U.S. capital?
   A. New York
   B. California
   C. Washington, D.C.
   D. Florida

3. What are the two major political parties in the U.S.?
   A. Senators and Representatives
   B. Democratic and Republican
   C. Stars and Stripes
   D. Federal and National

4. What is the head executive of a state called?
   A. a mayor
   B. a president
   C. a Republican
   D. a governor

5. What's the name of the national anthem of the U.S.?
   A. "The Red, White, and Blue"
   B. "The Stars and Stripes"
   C. "The Star-Spangled Banner"
   D. "The United States of America"

6. How many states are in the United States?
   A. 13 states
   B. 100 states
   C. 52 states
   D. 50 states

```
1. Ⓐ Ⓑ Ⓒ Ⓓ      4. Ⓐ Ⓑ Ⓒ Ⓓ
2. Ⓐ Ⓑ Ⓒ Ⓓ      5. Ⓐ Ⓑ Ⓒ Ⓓ
3. Ⓐ Ⓑ Ⓒ Ⓓ      6. Ⓐ Ⓑ Ⓒ Ⓓ
```

Writing Test 📼

1. _____

2. _____

3. _____

4. _____

5. _____

2. America's Early History

The **first** people to live in America were **Native Americans.**

Spelling	What Does It Mean?
America _____	Native Americans = Indians
live _____	first = number 1
first _____	

U.S. Holiday

We honor Christopher Columbus every year. Columbus Day is in October.

OCTOBER						
S	M	T	W	T	F	S
					1	2
3	4	5	6	7	8	9
10	11	12	13	14	15	16
17	18	19	20	21	22	23
24/31	25	26	27	28	29	30

Christopher Columbus came to America in 1492.

He came to America on a **ship.**

Spelling

Columbus _____

October _____

What Does It Mean?

honor = remember someone important

ship =

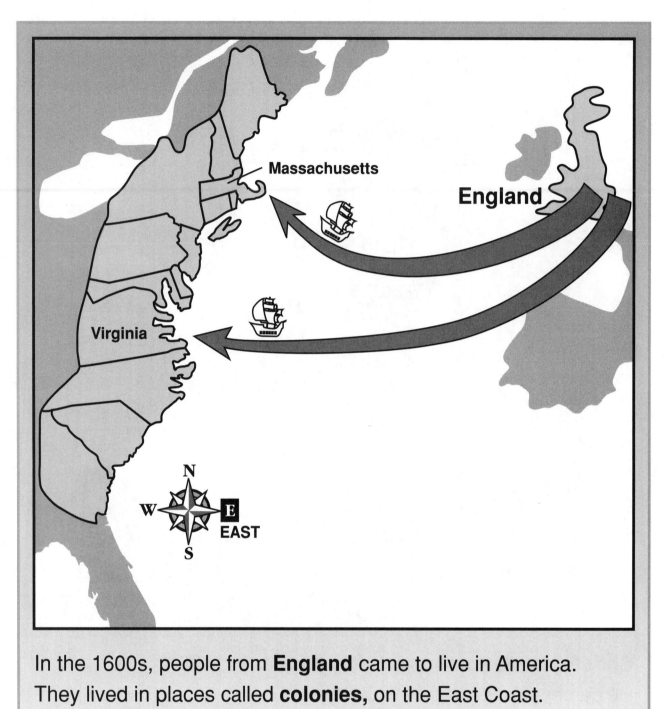

Massachusetts

England

Virginia

N
W
E
EAST
S

In the 1600s, people from **England** came to live in America.
They lived in places called **colonies,** on the East Coast.
The first colonies were Massachusetts and Virginia.

What Does It Mean?

colonies = places where people start new
    homes

coast = land next to the sea

east =

Some of the new **colonists** were called **Pilgrims.**

The Pilgrims came to America on a ship.

The name of the ship was the **Mayflower.**

Spelling

name _____

some _____

What Does It Mean?

colonists = people who lived in the colonies

The Pilgrims came to America because they wanted to be **free.**
In England, they could not choose their own church.
They came to America for **religious freedom.**

Spelling	**What Does It Mean?**
freedom _____	religious = the way people think about God or the way they pray
because _____	

The Native Americans helped the Pilgrims.

The Pilgrims **celebrated** the first **Thanksgiving.** They were happy to be alive after their first year in America.

U.S. Holiday

We celebrate Thanksgiving every year in November.

NOVEMBER						
S	M	T	W	T	F	S
		1	2	3	4	5	6
7	8	9	10	11	12	13
14	15	16	17	18	19	20
21	22	23	24	25	26	27
28	29	30				

Spelling

help _____

Thanksgiving _____

happy _____

What Does It Mean?

celebrate = get together on a special day

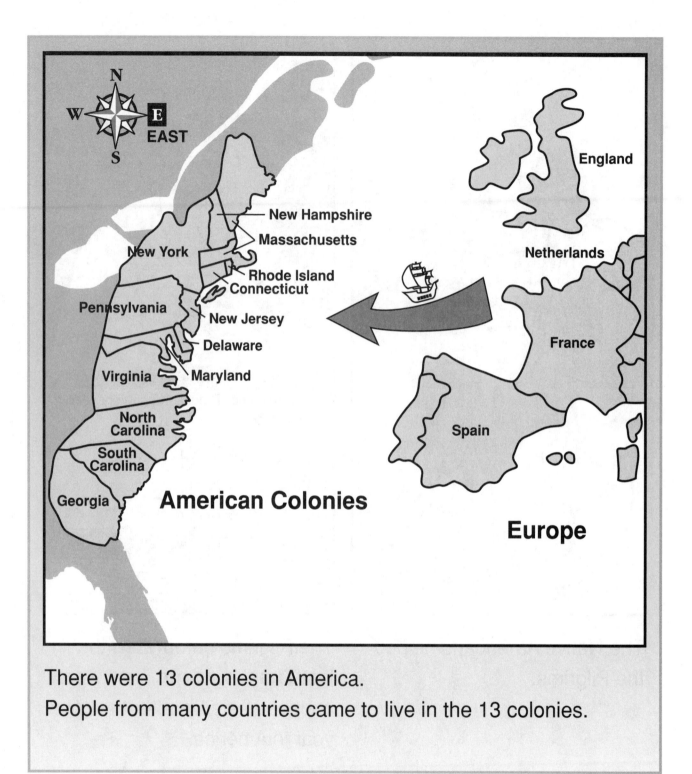

There were 13 colonies in America.

People from many countries came to live in the 13 colonies.

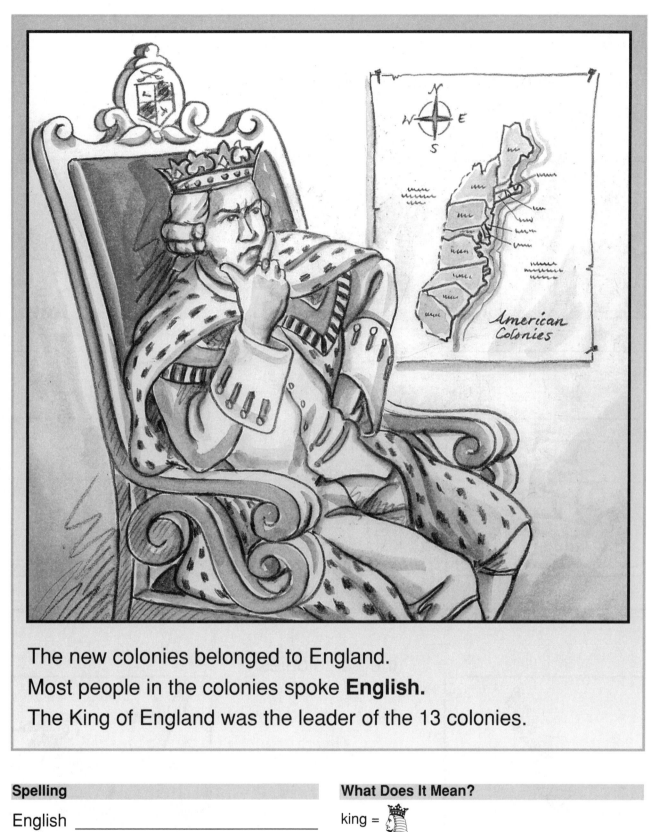

The new colonies belonged to England.

Most people in the colonies spoke **English.**

The King of England was the leader of the 13 colonies.

Spelling

English _____

most _____

What Does It Mean?

king =

Match

Find the words that go with the pictures.
Copy the words on the lines.

ship

Native
Americans

Christopher
Columbus

Pilgrims

the 13 colonies

England

1. _____

2. _____

3. _____

4. _____

5. _____

6. _____

What Does It Mean?

1. coast

2. the Mayflower

3. colonies

4. religious

5. celebrate

6. Native Americans

- the Pilgrims' ship

- the way people think about God

- Indians

- get together on a special day

- land next to the sea

- places where people start new homes

Yes or No?

yes   no   1. The first people to live in America were Native Americans.

yes   no   2. Christopher Columbus sailed to America in 1942.

yes   no   3. Christopher Columbus sailed to America on the Mayflower.

yes   no   4. Some new colonists from England were called Pilgrims.

yes   no   5. The Pilgrims came to America for religious freedom.

yes   no   6. The Pilgrims celebrated the first Thanksgiving.

yes   no   7. Native Americans helped the King of England.

yes   no   8. England had 13 colonies on the West Coast.

yes   no   9. Many people in the new colonies spoke English.

yes   no   10. Columbus Day is in July.

Spelling

A. Fill in the missing letters for words in this lesson.

1. Am__rica
2. C__lumb__s Day
3. Engl__sh
4. fir__t
5. fre__dom
6. he__ped
7. liv__
8. Oct__ber
9. Th__nksg__ving

B. Now use the same words to fill in the blanks.

1. Native Americans were the _____ people to live in America.

2. Christopher Columbus came to _____ in 1492.

3. _____ _____ is in October.

4. The Pilgrims came to America for religious _____ .

5. The Pilgrims celebrated the first _____ .

6. Most of the new colonists spoke _____ .

Say the Answer

1. Why did the Pilgrims come to America?

2. What is the name of the ship that brought the Pilgrims to America?

3. Who helped the Pilgrims in America?

4. What holiday was celebrated for the first time by the American colonists?

Writing Cards Set 2

6. Columbus Day is in October.

_____

_____

7. We live in America.

_____

_____

8. Thanksgiving is in November.

_____

_____

9. I can speak English.

_____

_____

10. I can read and write English.

_____

_____

Test Hint #2

If you need to, it's OK to ask the examiner to repeat a question.

If you don't understand a question, it's OK to ask the examiner to say it again. Say:

Excuse me, would you repeat the question?

Fill in the missing words:

Excuse me, _____ you repeat the _____?
Excuse _____, would you _____ the question?
_____ _____, would you _____ _____ question?

If you can't hear the question, it's OK to ask the examiner to speak louder. Say:

Excuse me, would you say it louder?

Fill in the missing words:

Excuse me, would you _____ it louder?
_____ me, would _____ say it _____ ?
Excuse me, _____ you _____ _____ louder?

Try the Test

Mark the answer box with the best answer for each question.

1. Who lived in America before the Pilgrims came?
   A. Christopher Columbus
   B. George Washington
   C. Native Americans
   D. the King of England

2. What was the name of the ship that brought the Pilgrims to America?
   A. the New York
   B. the Constitution
   C. the Titanic
   D. the Mayflower

3. How many original colonies were in America?
   A. 13
   B. 50
   C. 17
   D. 200

4. Who helped the Pilgrims when they came to America?
   A. Christopher Columbus
   B. Native Americans
   C. the King of England
   D. the Europeans

5. What holiday was celebrated for the first time by the American colonists?
   A. Independence Day
   B. Columbus Day
   C. Presidents' Day
   D. Thanksgiving

6. Why did the Pilgrims come to America?
   A. for religious freedom
   B. to help the Native Americans
   C. to celebrate a holiday
   D. to help the King of England

1. Ⓐ Ⓑ Ⓒ Ⓓ   4. Ⓐ Ⓑ Ⓒ Ⓓ
2. Ⓐ Ⓑ Ⓒ Ⓓ   5. Ⓐ Ⓑ Ⓒ Ⓓ
3. Ⓐ Ⓑ Ⓒ Ⓓ   6. Ⓐ Ⓑ Ⓒ Ⓓ

Writing Test 📼

6. _____

7. _____

8. _____

9. _____

10. _____

3. The Revolutionary War

In the 1770s, the **colonists** were angry at the King of England.

They thought the English **laws** were **unfair.**

They did not want the king to be their leader.

They wanted to elect their own leaders.

What Does It Mean?

colonists = people who lived in the 13 colonies

Patrick Henry was one of the angry colonists.
He wanted to live in a free country.

free _____

Patrick Henry said, "Give me **liberty** or give me death."

Spelling	**What Does It Mean?**
liberty _____	liberty = freedom

Many colonists agreed with Patrick Henry.
They said America did not belong to England anymore.
They said that America was now an **independent** country.

Spelling

country _____

now _____

What Does It Mean?

independent = free (not part of another country)

The King of England did not want the colonies to be independent. He sent his **army** to America to stop the colonists.

Spelling

sent _____

What Does It Mean?

army =

The American colonists fought a **war** against England.
It was called the **Revolutionary War.**

Spelling	What Does It Mean?
war _____	revolution = change to a different government
	war = a fight between two countries

During the war, the colonists put their ideas in a paper.
Thomas Jefferson wrote the paper for the colonists.
It was called the **Declaration of Independence.**

Spelling

independence _____

put _____

What Does It Mean?

declaration = a paper that tells everyone what
    you've decided

independence = freedom

Jefferson wrote, "**All men are created equal.**"
This means that all people have the same **rights.**
This is a **basic belief** of the Declaration of Independence.

What Does It Mean?

created = made by God

equal = the same

rights = things the government lets you do

basic belief = important idea

The leaders of all 13 colonies agreed with the ideas in the Declaration of Independence.

They **adopted** the Declaration of Independence on July 4, 1776.

Spelling

July _____

with _____

all _____

What Does It Mean?

adopted = voted yes

U.S. Holiday

We celebrate Independence Day on July 4 every year.

JULY						
S	M	T	W	T	F	S
				1	2	3
4	5	6	7	8	9	10
11	12	13	14	15	16	17
18	19	20	21	22	23	24
25	26	27	28	29	30	31

July 4, 1776, is the birthday of the United States.
We call it Independence Day.

Spelling

birthday _____

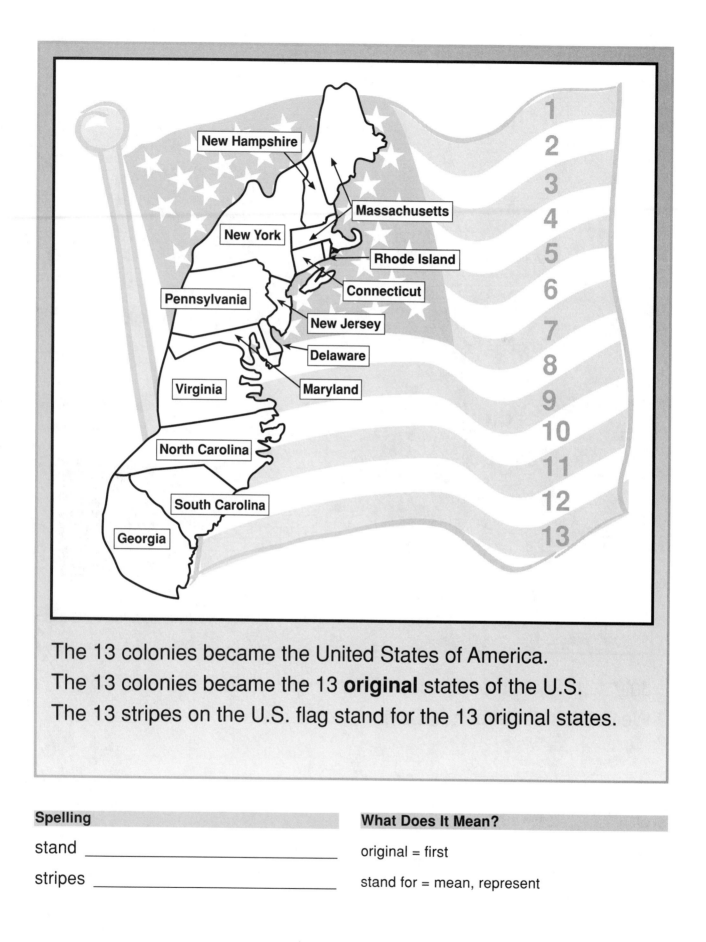

The 13 colonies became the United States of America.

The 13 colonies became the 13 **original** states of the U.S.

The 13 stripes on the U.S. flag stand for the 13 original states.

Spelling	What Does It Mean?
stand _____	original = first
stripes _____	stand for = mean, represent

The leader of the Colonial Army was **George Washington.**
George Washington was the **commander in chief** of the army.
George Washington helped the colonists win the Revolutionary
  War.

Spelling	**What Does It Mean?**
George	commander in chief = army leader
Washington _____	

After the Revolutionary War, George Washington became the first U.S. president.

Spelling

president _____

U.S. Holiday

We celebrate George Washington's birthday on Presidents' Day. Presidents' Day is in February.

FEBRUARY						
S	M	T	W	T	F	S
		1	2	3	4	5	6
7	8	9	10	11	12	13
14	15	16	17	18	19	20
21	22	23	24	25	26	27
28						

Now George Washington is called "the father of our country."

Spelling

father _____

our _____

February _____

Match

Find the words that go with the pictures.
Copy the words on the lines.

1. _____

2. _____

3. _____

war

army

Independence Day

Declaration of
Independence

stripes

George Washington

4. _____

5. _____

6. _____

What Does It Mean?

1. commander in chief

2. Revolutionary War

3. independent

4. "All men are created equal."

5. basic belief

- not part of another country

- army leader

- important idea

- war between England and America

- All people have the same rights.

Yes or No?

yes   no   1. In 1776, the colonists wanted America to be part of England.

yes   no   2. George Washington wrote the Declaration of Independence.

yes   no   3. Thomas Jefferson wrote the Declaration of Independence.

yes   no   4. The Declaration of Independence was adopted in 1776.

yes   no   5. In 1776, the 13 colonies became the United States.

yes   no   6. The American colonists fought a war against the Pilgrims.

yes   no   7. George Washington was the commander in chief of the Colonial Army.

yes   no   8. England won the Revolutionary War.

yes   no   9. Thomas Jefferson was the first president of the U.S.

Spelling

A. Fill in the missing letters for words in this lesson.

1. b__rthd__y
2. coun__ry
3. f__ther

4. Feb__uar__
5. Ind__pende__ce
6. J__ly

7. pr__side__t
8. stan__
9. st__ipes

B. Now use the same words to fill in the blanks.

1. The father of our _____ is George Washington.

2. Washington's birthday is in _____ .

3. The stripes on the flag _____ for the 13 original states.

4. _____ Day is in July.

5. The flag has 13 _____ .

6. George Washington was the first U.S. _____ .

7. July 4, 1776, is the _____ of the United States.

Say the Answer

1. What were the 13 original states called before they were states?

2. Can you name some of the 13 original states?

3. Who was the first president of the U.S.?

4. What do the stripes on the flag represent?

5. Who said, "Give me liberty or give me death"?

6. What do we celebrate on July 4?

Writing Cards Set 3

11. George Washington is the father of our country.

_____

_____

12. The birthday of the U.S. is July 4.

_____

_____

13. George Washington was the first U.S. president.

_____

_____

14. Independence Day is in July.

_____

_____

15. The U.S. flag has 13 stripes.

_____

_____

Test Hint #3

There are many ways to ask the same question.

Who was the first president of the United States?

If you know the answer, try these questions too:

- Do you know the name of the first U.S. president?
- Name the first president of the United States.
- Can you tell me the name of the first U.S. president?
- What was the name of the first president?

These are different forms of the same question.
They are different ways to ask the same question.

All of the questions have the same KEY words: **first** and **president.**
The key words are the important words in the question.
All of the questions have the same answer.

Since you can't know which form the examiner will ask,

- practice many forms of the same question
- listen for the key words each time

Try the Test

Mark the answer box with the best answer for each question.

1. Who was the first commander in chief of the U.S. military?
   A. Christopher Columbus
   B. the King of England
   C. Thomas Jefferson
   D. George Washington

2. What is a basic belief of the Declaration of Independence?
   A. The Pilgrims should have religious freedom.
   B. All people are created equal.
   C. The 13 colonies were part of England.
   D. Native Americans should have their own leaders.

3. What war did the American colonists fight against England?
   A. the American Civil War
   B. World War I
   C. the Revolutionary War
   D. the French and Indian War

4. Why did the colonists go to war with England?
   A. They thought the English laws were unfair.
   B. They wanted religious freedom.
   C. They wanted Thomas Jefferson to be king.
   D. They did not like the English flag.

5. Who was the main writer of the Declaration of Independence?
   A. Christopher Columbus
   B. Abraham Lincoln
   C. George Washington
   D. Thomas Jefferson

6. When was the Declaration of Independence adopted?
   A. July 7, 1976
   B. January 1, 1776
   C. July 4, 1776
   D. June 6, 1776

1. Ⓐ Ⓑ Ⓒ Ⓓ	4. Ⓐ Ⓑ Ⓒ Ⓓ
2. Ⓐ Ⓑ Ⓒ Ⓓ	5. Ⓐ Ⓑ Ⓒ Ⓓ
3. Ⓐ Ⓑ Ⓒ Ⓓ	6. Ⓐ Ⓑ Ⓒ Ⓓ

Writing Test 📼

11. _____

12. _____

13. _____

14. _____

15. _____

4. The Civil War

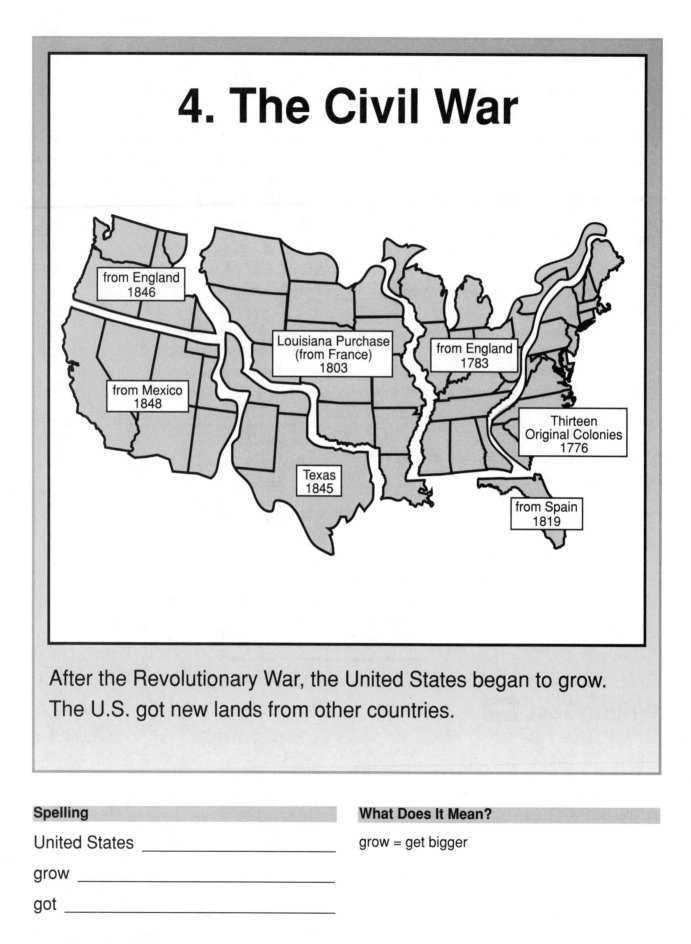

After the Revolutionary War, the United States began to grow. The U.S. got new lands from other countries.

Spelling

United States _____

grow _____

got _____

What Does It Mean?

grow = get bigger

For many years, Americans used **slaves** to work on their farms and in their homes.
The slaves were from Africa.

work _____

What Does It Mean?

slave = someone who is owned by another person

In the 1860s, Americans in the **North** said slavery was not OK.

They thought the slaves should be **free.**

They made laws to stop **slavery.**

Spelling

free _____

stop _____

What Does It Mean?

free = not slaves anymore

slavery = owning slaves

North =

But Americans in the **South** did not agree.

They wanted to keep their slaves.

They did not like the new laws against slavery.

Spelling

South _____

like _____

What Does It Mean?

agree = say "OK"

South =

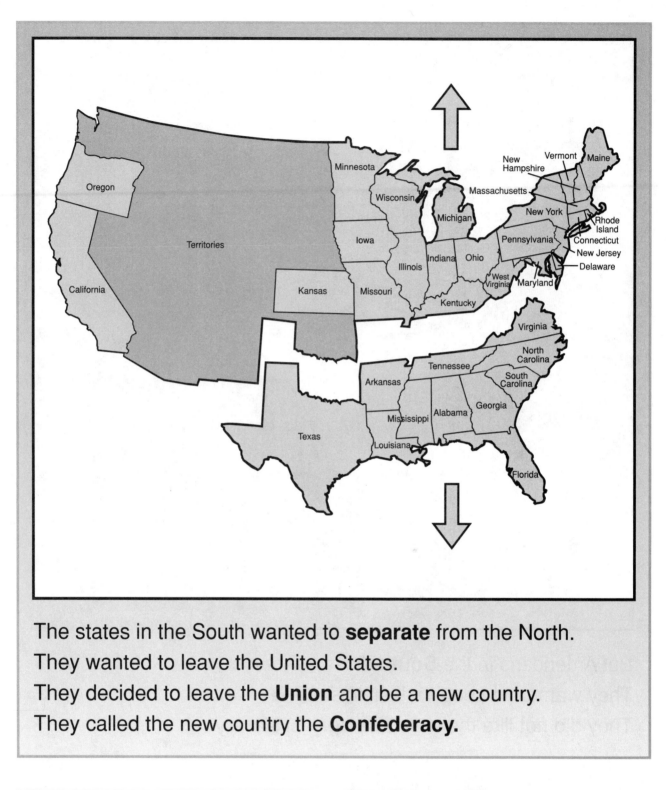

The states in the South wanted to **separate** from the North.

They wanted to leave the United States.

They decided to leave the **Union** and be a new country.

They called the new country the **Confederacy.**

Spelling

Union _____

What Does It Mean?

separate = not be together anymore

Union = the United States

The North did not want the South to leave the Union.

The North and the South fought against each other in a war.

This was called the **Civil War.**

Spelling

Civil War _____

this _____

The president during the Civil War was **Abraham Lincoln.**
He wanted to keep the North and South together.

Spelling

keep _____

North _____

Emancipation Proclamation

Abraham Lincoln signed a paper called the **Emancipation Proclamation.**

The Emancipation Proclamation freed the slaves.

Abraham Lincoln freed the slaves.

Spelling

paper _____

Abraham
Lincoln _____

What Does It Mean?

signed = put his name on

The Union Army won the war in 1865.
The United States stayed together.
President Lincoln **saved the Union.**

Spelling

won _____

saved _____

What Does It Mean?

save the Union = keep all the U.S. states
   together

U.S. Holiday

We celebrate Lincoln's birthday with Washington's birthday. The holiday is called Presidents' Day. Presidents' Day is in February.

FEBRUARY						
S	M	T	W	T	F	S
	1	2	3	4	5	6
7	8	9	10	11	12	13
14	15	16	17	18	19	20
21	22	23	24	25	26	27
28						

Abraham Lincoln was killed at the end of the war.

Americans remember Abraham Lincoln because he helped the U.S. at a hard time.

Spelling

hard _____

time _____

Match

Find the words that go with the pictures.
Copy the words on the lines.

slaves

North

South

Abraham
Lincoln

Civil War

signed

1. _____

2. _____

3. _____

4. _____

5. _____

6. _____

What Does It Mean?

1. separate
2. save the Union
3. free
4. Emancipation Proclamation
5. agree
6. grow

- keep all the states together
- say "OK"
- not together
- a paper to free the slaves
- get bigger
- not slaves

Yes or No?

yes   no   1. Abraham Lincoln was president during the Revolutionary War.

yes   no   2. The states in the South wanted to stop slavery.

yes   no   3. The states in the South wanted to leave the Union.

yes   no   4. The states in the North wanted to keep the Union.

yes   no   5. Abraham Lincoln wanted to keep the North and South together.

yes   no   6. The U.S. got new lands from other countries after the Revolutionary War.

yes   no   7. Thomas Jefferson signed the Emancipation Proclamation.

yes   no   8. We celebrate Abraham Lincoln's birthday in July.

yes   no   9. Abraham Lincoln freed the slaves.

Spelling

A. Fill in the missing letters for words in this lesson.

1. Abr__ham Li__coln
2. Ci__il W__r
3. fr__e
4. gro__

5. N__rth
6. sav__d
7. Sout__
8. wo__k

9. U__ion
10. Un__ted St__tes
11. w__n
12. pap__r

B. Now use the same words to fill in the blanks.

1. During the _____ _____ , Lincoln was president.

2. A slave is a person who is not _____ .

3. People in the _____ wanted to keep their slaves.

4. Abraham Lincoln saved the _____ .

5. The North _____ the Civil War.

6. _____ _____ signed the Emancipation

   Proclamation.

7. The U.S. began to _____ after the Revolutionary
   War.

Say the Answer

1. Who was president during the Civil War?
2. What did the Emancipation Proclamation do?
3. Which president freed the slaves?

Writing Cards Set 4

16. The United States is a free country.

_____

_____

17. Abraham Lincoln saved the Union.

_____

_____

18. The North won the Civil War.

_____

_____

19. Presidents' Day is in February.

_____

_____

20. We live in North America.

_____

_____

Test Hint #4

Different INS examiners may give the test in different ways.

One examiner may ask you to listen to questions. Another examiner may ask you to read questions from a list. For example:

Please read question number three and tell me the answer.

An examiner may also ask you to write the answer. For example:

Please read question number four and write the answer here.

Practice three different ways so you will be ready for any test:

Read questions and write the answers.

Read questions and speak the answers.

Listen to questions and speak the answers.

Try the Test

Mark the answer box with the best answer for each question.

1. Who was president during the Civil War?
   A. George Washington
   B. Abraham Lincoln
   C. General Grant
   D. Thomas Jefferson

2. Why do we remember Abraham Lincoln?
   A. He freed the slaves and saved the Union.
   B. He was the first colonist to come to America.
   C. He wrote the Declaration of Independence.
   D. He was the first president of the U.S.

3. What is the name of the American war fought in the 1860s?
   A. World War II
   B. the Revolutionary War
   C. the French and Indian War
   D. the Civil War

4. What was the main reason for the Civil War?
   A. slavery
   B. religious freedom
   C. high taxes
   D. problems with England

5. Who signed the Emancipation Proclamation?
   A. the slaves
   B. leaders from the South
   C. Abraham Lincoln
   D. Thomas Jefferson

6. What did the Emancipation Proclamation do?
   A. freed slaves
   B. made Abraham Lincoln president
   C. made the South a separate country
   D. started the Civil War

```
1. Ⓐ Ⓑ Ⓒ Ⓓ      4. Ⓐ Ⓑ Ⓒ Ⓓ
2. Ⓐ Ⓑ Ⓒ Ⓓ      5. Ⓐ Ⓑ Ⓒ Ⓓ
3. Ⓐ Ⓑ Ⓒ Ⓓ      6. Ⓐ Ⓑ Ⓒ Ⓓ
```

Writing Test

16. _____

17. _____

18. _____

19. _____

20. _____

5. Later History

After the Civil War, **millions** of **immigrants** came to the U.S. The U.S. **population grew.**

Spelling

after _____

came _____

What Does It Mean?

millions = more than 1,000,000

population = number of people

grew = got bigger

immigrants = new settlers, people who came to live in a new place

From 1917 to 1918, the U.S. fought against Germany in **World War I.**

Franklin D. Roosevelt

In 1929 the **Great Depression** began.

Many people did not have work.

President **Franklin D. Roosevelt** helped Americans during the Depression.

Spelling

Americans _____

From 1941 to 1945, the U.S. fought **World War II.**

The U.S. fought against Germany, Japan, and Italy.

In World War II, Germany, Japan, and Italy were **enemies** of the U.S.

What Does It Mean?

enemies = countries we fought against

The U.S. did not fight the war alone.

Other countries helped.

England, France, and Russia helped the U.S.

Spelling

fight _____

U.S. Holidays

Memorial Day is in May. Veterans Day is in November.

		NOVEMBER				
S	M	T	W	T	F	S
		1	2	3	4	5	6
7	8	9	10	11	12	13
14	15	16	17	18	19	20
				25	26	27

		MAY				
S	M	T	W	T	F	S
1	2	3	4	5	6	7
8	9	10	11	12	13	14
15	16	17	18	19	20	21
22	23	24	25	26	27	28
29	30	31				

We honor the Americans who fought in U.S. wars.
Memorial Day and Veterans Day are national holidays.

Spelling

Veterans Day _____

Memorial Day _____

honor _____

May _____

What Does It Mean?

honor = remember, say "thank you"

veteran = someone who was a soldier

memorial = a time to remember

After World War II, the U.S. and other countries started the
United Nations.
The reason for the United Nations is to **keep peace** in the world.

Spelling	What Does It Mean?
nation _____	nation = country
peace _____	

At the United Nations, countries talk about their problems together.
They try to fix their problems.
This is one **purpose** of the United Nations.
Countries **discuss** and try to **resolve** problems.

Spelling

try _____

fix _____

talk _____

together _____

What Does It Mean?

purpose = reason

discuss = talk about

resolve = fix

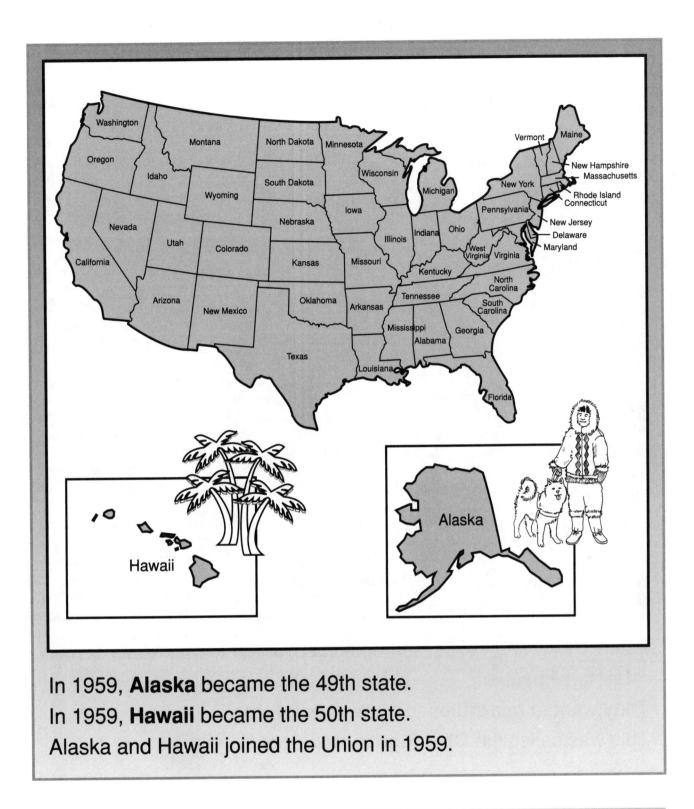

In 1959, **Alaska** became the 49th state.

In 1959, **Hawaii** became the 50th state.

Alaska and Hawaii joined the Union in 1959.

What Does It Mean?

joined the Union = became part of the U.S.

In the 1960s and 1970s, some people wanted to make U.S. laws
   fair to all people.

They wanted **minorities** to have **equal rights.**

This was called the **Civil Rights movement.**

Spelling

rights _____

have _____

fair _____

What Does It Mean?

fair = the same for everybody

equal rights = the same rights for all people

minorities =

U.S. Holiday

Dr. King's birthday is a national holiday. Martin Luther King Jr. Day is in January.

JANUARY

S	M	T	W	T	F	S
					1	2
3	4	5	6	7	8	9
10	11	12	13	14	15	16
17	18	19	20	21	22	23
24/31	25	26	27	28	29	30

Dr. **Martin Luther King Jr.** was a leader in the Civil Rights movement.

He was a civil rights leader in the 1960s.

Spelling

national _____

holiday _____

leader _____

Match

Find the words that go with the pictures.
Copy the words on the lines.

minorities

United Nations

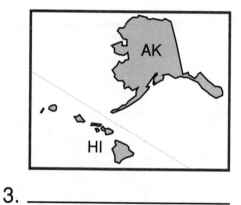

1. _____

3. _____

Martin Luther King Jr.

Alaska and Hawaii

immigrants

2. _____

4. _____

5. _____

What Does It Mean?

1. enemies

2. purpose

3. equal rights

4. population

5. millions

6. discuss

7. grew

8. resolve

- the same rights for everybody
- countries the U.S. fought against
- talk about
- fix
- number of people
- got bigger
- more than 1,000,000
- reason

Yes or No?

yes no 1. After the Civil War, the U.S. population grew.

yes no 2. The population grew because millions of immigrants came to the U.S.

yes no 3. In World War II, the U.S. fought against England.

yes no 4. In World War II, Germany and Japan were enemies of the U.S.

yes no 5. The U.S. fought against Germany in World War I.

yes no 6. In 1959, Florida became the 50th state.

yes no 7. Dr. Martin Luther King Jr. was a leader in World War II.

yes no 8. Dr. Martin Luther King Jr. was a civil rights leader.

Spelling

A. Fill in the missing letters for words in this lesson.

1. Am__ricans
2. h__liday
3. hon__r

4. lead__r
5. __ame
6. Memo__ial Day

7. ta__k
8. righ__s
9. Vet__rans Day

B. Now use the same words to fill in the blanks.

1. After the Civil War, many immigrants _____ to the U.S.

2. We _____ Americans who fought in U.S. wars.

3. _____ _____ is in May.

4. Martin Luther King Jr. Day is a national _____ .

5. Dr. Martin Luther King Jr. was a _____ in the Civil Rights movement.

6. All Americans have _____ .

7. Countries _____ together at the United Nations.

Say the Answer

1. Name one purpose of the United Nations.
2. Name some countries that were our enemies during World War II.
3. What were the 49th and 50th states added to our Union?
4. Who was Martin Luther King Jr.?

Writing Cards Set 5

21. Americans live in freedom.

_____

_____

22. All Americans have rights.

_____

_____

23. Memorial Day is in May.

_____

_____

24. Veterans Day is in November.

_____

_____

25. The United States has 50 states.

_____

_____

Test Hint #5

Nobody is perfect. If you forget an answer, you can still pass the test.

What will you do if you can't remember an answer?

Don't get upset.
It's OK to say, "I don't remember."
The examiner will ask another question.

If you remember one part of the answer, tell the examiner the part you remember.
For example:

Examiner:

What were the 49th and 50th states to join our Union?

Applicant:

Hawaii and . . . I can't remember the other one.

If you can answer most of the questions, you can still pass the test.

Try the Test

Mark the answer box with the best answer for each question.

1. Which countries helped the U.S. in World War II?
   A. Germany and Japan
   B. England, France, and Russia
   C. Mexico and Spain
   D. Italy, Greece, and Turkey

2. Who was Martin Luther King Jr.?
   A. a leader in the Civil War
   B. a general in the U.S. Army
   C. a civil rights leader
   D. the first U.S. president

3. Which war did the U.S. fight from 1941 to 1945?
   A. World War I
   B. World War II
   C. the Vietnam War
   D. the Civil War

4. Who were enemies of the U.S. in World War II?
   A. France and England
   B. Korea and Vietnam
   C. Mexico and Canada
   D. Germany and Japan

5. What were the 49th and 50th states added to our Union?
   A. Alaska and Hawaii
   B. Maine and Florida
   C. California and Texas
   D. Florida and New York

6. What is one thing countries do at the United Nations?
   A. try to resolve problems
   B. fight against their enemies
   C. talk about World War II
   D. make new political parties

1. Ⓐ Ⓑ Ⓒ Ⓓ   4. Ⓐ Ⓑ Ⓒ Ⓓ
2. Ⓐ Ⓑ Ⓒ Ⓓ   5. Ⓐ Ⓑ Ⓒ Ⓓ
3. Ⓐ Ⓑ Ⓒ Ⓓ   6. Ⓐ Ⓑ Ⓒ Ⓓ

Writing Test

21. _____

22. _____

23. _____

24. _____

25. _____

History Review

People to Remember

Christopher Columbus   George Washington   Thomas Jefferson   the King of England   Abraham Lincoln   Martin Luther King Jr.

1. He wrote the Declaration of Independence. _Thomas Jefferson_

2. He sent his army to fight the American colonists.

   _____

3. He was a civil rights leader in the 1960s. _____

4. He freed the slaves and saved the Union. _____

5. He became the first president of the U.S. _____

6. He came to America in 1492. _____

Groups to Remember

Native Americans

Pilgrims

the Colonial Army

immigrants

the United Nations

U.S. minorities

1. Countries try to resolve problems together. _____

2. They helped the new colonists. _____

3. They came to America from many countries. _____

4. It fought against England in the Revolutionary War.

   _____

5. Martin Luther King Jr. helped them to get equal rights.

   _____

6. They celebrated the first Thanksgiving.

   _____

When Did It Happen?

Here are some important things that happened in U.S. history.
Put them on the right date on the time line.

- The U.S. fought in World War II.

- Columbus came to America.

- The 13 colonies became the United States.

- Martin Luther King Jr. helped minorities.

- Hawaii joined the Union.

- The first colonists from England came to America.

- The North and the South fought in the Civil War.

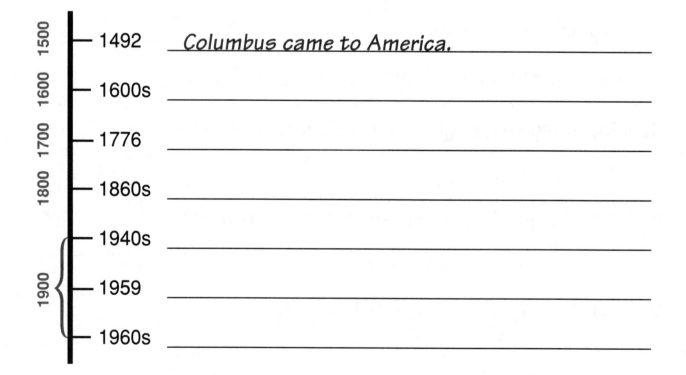

— 1492	_Columbus came to America._
— 1600s	
— 1776	
— 1860s	
— 1940s	
— 1959	
— 1960s	

When Is the Holiday?

Find the right holiday. Then finish the sentences and copy them.

- Independence Day
- Martin Luther King Jr. ✓
  Day
- Columbus Day
- Thanksgiving
- Presidents' Day
- Memorial Day

1. _____Thanksgiving_____ is in November.

   _____Thanksgiving is in November._____

2. _____ is in July.

   _____

3. _____ is in February.

   _____

4. _____ is in _____ .

   _____

5. _____ .

   _____

6. _____ .

   _____

History Test A

Mark the answer box with the best answer for each question.

1. Which president is called "the father of our country"?
   A. Abraham Lincoln
   B. George Washington
   C. Thomas Jefferson
   D. Franklin Roosevelt

2. Which two states were the last to join the Union?
   A. Alaska and Hawaii
   B. Florida and New York
   C. California and Oregon
   D. Maine and Maryland

3. Which president freed the slaves and saved the Union?
   A. John F. Kennedy
   B. George Washington
   C. Thomas Jefferson
   D. Abraham Lincoln

4. When did the U.S. fight the Civil War?
   A. in the 1860s
   B. in the 1960s
   C. in the 1770s
   D. in the 1660s

5. The 13 colonies fought against England in what war?
   A. the Civil War
   B. the Revolutionary War
   C. World War II
   D. the Vietnam War

6. Who celebrated Thanksgiving for the first time in America?
   A. the Pilgrims
   B. the Confederate Army
   C. the slaves
   D. the Colonial Army

7. What is the head executive of a city called?
   A. a president
   B. a mayor
   C. a governor
   D. a senator

8. What do the stripes on the flag stand for?
   A. the original 13 states
   B. 13 men who signed the Declaration of Independence
   C. 13 years of war
   D. 13 men who fought in the Civil War

1. Ⓐ Ⓑ Ⓒ Ⓓ	5. Ⓐ Ⓑ Ⓒ Ⓓ
2. Ⓐ Ⓑ Ⓒ Ⓓ	6. Ⓐ Ⓑ Ⓒ Ⓓ
3. Ⓐ Ⓑ Ⓒ Ⓓ	7. Ⓐ Ⓑ Ⓒ Ⓓ
4. Ⓐ Ⓑ Ⓒ Ⓓ	8. Ⓐ Ⓑ Ⓒ Ⓓ

Writing Test 🖭

A. _____

B. _____

History Test B

Mark the circle next to the best answer for each question.

1. What was the purpose of the Emancipation Proclamation?
   - ○ A. to start a war
   - ○ B. to make the South separate from the North
   - ○ C. to free the slaves
   - ○ D. to make Abraham Lincoln president

2. What is George Washington famous for?
   - ○ A. He was the first U.S. president.
   - ○ B. He came to America with the Pilgrims.
   - ○ C. He fought in the Civil War.
   - ○ D. He wrote the Declaration of Independence.

3. What do we celebrate on July 4?
   - ○ A. New Year's Day
   - ○ B. Columbus Day
   - ○ C. Thanksgiving
   - ○ D. Independence Day

4. What is the capital of the United States?
   - ○ A. New York
   - ○ B. Washington, D.C.
   - ○ C. Philadelphia
   - ○ D. Boston

5. Who signed the Emancipation Proclamation?
   - ○ A. Abraham Lincoln
   - ○ B. the King of England
   - ○ C. George Washington
   - ○ D. Martin Luther King Jr.

6. How many U.S. states are there?
   - ○ A. 13
   - ○ B. 50
   - ○ C. 100
   - ○ D. 52

7. What country did we fight in the Revolutionary War?
   - ○ A. Japan
   - ○ B. Germany
   - ○ C. Vietnam
   - ○ D. England

8. Which countries helped the U.S. in World War II?
   - ○ A. France, England, and Russia
   - ○ B. Mexico, Spain, and Colombia
   - ○ C. Vietnam and Korea
   - ○ D. Italy and Germany

9. What do the stars on the flag mean?
   - ○ A. one for each original colony
   - ○ B. one for each president
   - ○ C. one for each war we fought
   - ○ D. one for each state

10. How many stripes are on the U.S. flag?
    - ○ A. 10
    - ○ B. 50
    - ○ C. 13
    - ○ D. 16

Writing Test 🖭

A. _____

B. _____

6. The Constitution

Constitution

The **Constitution** tells how the U.S. government works.
It is the highest law of the U.S.
It is the **supreme law** of the land.

Spelling	What Does It Mean?
highest _____	highest = number 1
land _____	law = rule
law _____	supreme = most important

The Constitution was written in 1787.
All of the 13 original states accepted the Constitution.

Spelling

Constitution _____

What Does It Mean?

accepted = said "yes"

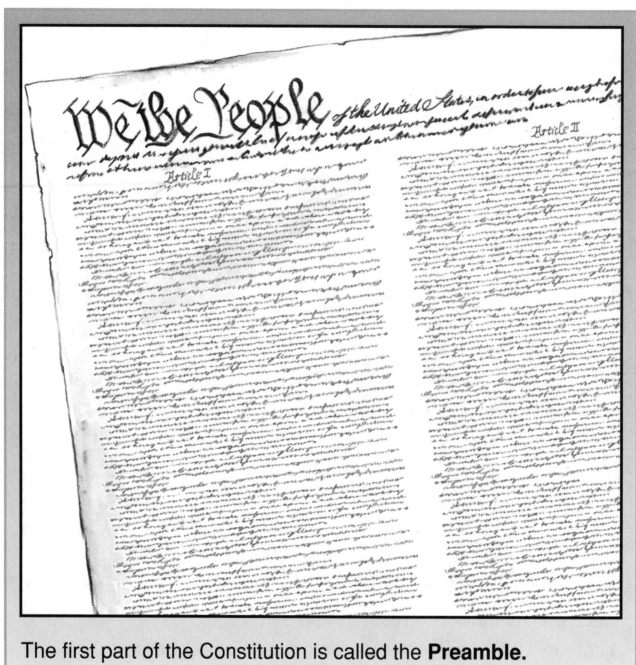

The first part of the Constitution is called the **Preamble.**
The Preamble is the introduction to the Constitution.

What Does It Mean?

preamble = first part

introduction = first part

The Constitution gives **basic rights** to all people living in the U.S. Under the Constitution, citizens and non-citizens all have rights.

Spelling

citizens _____

gives _____

What Does It Mean?

non-citizens = people who are not citizens

basic rights = things the government lets you do

under = as part of

Drive a car

Own a home or land

BAKER JUNIOR HIGH SCHOOL

Go to school

WATERHOUSE ASSEMBLY PLANT

GATE 2

Work

Non-citizens can do many things in the U.S.

Vote

Work for the U.S. Government

Travel with a U.S. Passport

Bring close relatives to live in the U.S.

But only U.S. **citizens** can do some things.
The pictures here show some **benefits** of being a U.S. citizen.

Spelling

vote _____

What Does It Mean?

benefits = special rights

relatives = family

The most important right **granted** to citizens is the right to vote.

Spelling	What Does It Mean?
important _____	granted = given

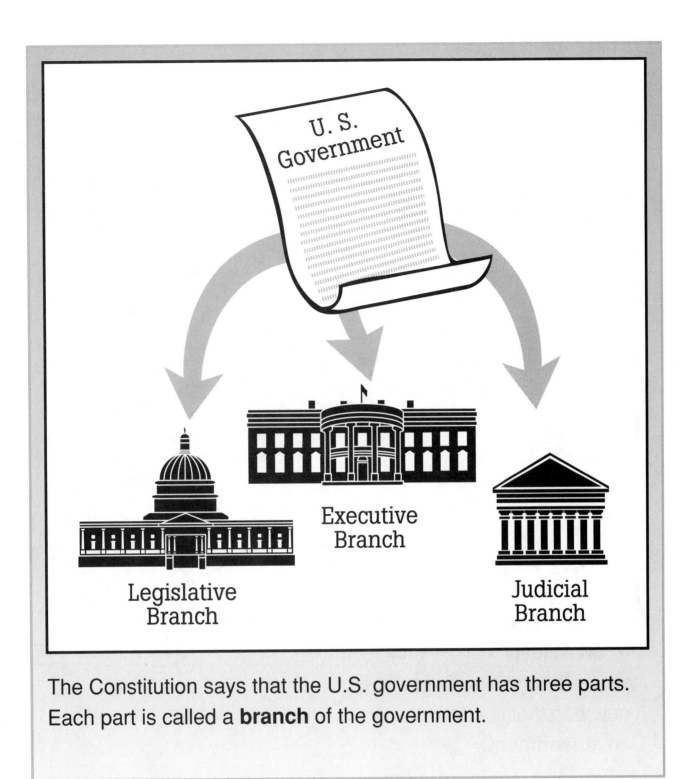

The Constitution says that the U.S. government has three parts. Each part is called a **branch** of the government.

What Does It Mean?

branch = main part of the government

The Constitution can be **changed**.

New parts can be added to it.

A new part that is added to the Constitution is called
  an **amendment**.

What Does It Mean?

change = make something different

amendment = a new part added to the
  Constitution

Ten amendments were added to the Constitution when it
was new.

These first 10 amendments are called the **Bill of Rights.**

The Bill of Rights is part of the Constitution.

Spelling

Bill of Rights _____

The Bill of Rights is important for all Americans.

It says that people can do many things.

People do not need to ask the government if it's OK.

The government cannot stop them.

Spelling

need _____

ask _____

things _____

Freedom of assembly

Freedom of speech

Freedom of the press

Freedom of religion

The **First Amendment** gives everyone important rights.
People can speak freely. They can write their ideas.
They can have peaceful meetings.
They can pray any way they like.

Spelling

speech _____

speak _____

everyone _____

What Does It Mean?

press = newspapers, radio, television

After the Bill of Rights, other amendments were added to the Constitution.

For example, the 14th, 15th, and 19th Amendments **guarantee** voting rights for all citizens.

Today there are 27 amendments to the Constitution.

Spelling

today ______________________________

Match

Find the words that go with the pictures.
Copy the words on the lines. Some words are used twice.

freedom of
speech

freedom of
religion

freedom of
the press

freedom of
assembly

1. _____

2. _____

3. _____

4. _____

5. _____

6. _____

What Does It Mean?

1. permission

2. freedom of speech

3. the Bill of Rights

4. the Constitution

5. amendment

6. highest

7. branches

- the first 10 amendments to the Constitution

- change to the Constitution

- The government says it's OK.

- number 1

- You can say what you want.

- parts of the government

- the highest law of the U.S.

Yes or No?

yes   no   1. The Constitution is the supreme law of the U.S.

yes   no   2. The Bill of Rights is the first 10 amendments to the Constitution.

yes   no   3. The Constitution was written in 1787.

yes   no   4. The Constitution says the U.S. government has 4 branches.

yes   no   5. The Constitution can never be changed.

yes   no   6. The Constitution gives rights to all people living in the U.S.

yes   no   7. A change to the Constitution is called a declaration.

yes   no   8. There are 27 amendments to the Constitution.

Spelling

A. Fill in the missing letters for words in this lesson.

1. B__ll of Ri__hts
4. giv__s
7. l__w

2. citi__ens
5. high__st
8. spe__ch

3. Con__tit__tion
6. lan__
9. vo__e

B. Now use the same words to fill in the blanks.

1. The _____ is the supreme law.

2. The first 10 amendments are the _____ _____
   _____ .

3. The Bill of Rights gives freedom of _____ to
   Americans.

4. The highest law of the _____ is the Constitution.

5. Only U.S. citizens can _____ .

6. All _____ have rights.

Say the Answer

1. Name one right guaranteed by the First Amendment.

2. Name one benefit of being a citizen of the U.S.

3. What is the most important right granted to U.S. citizens?

4. In what year was the Constitution written?

5. Whose rights are guaranteed by the Constitution?

6. What is the introduction to the Constitution called?

7. Name the amendments that guarantee voting rights.

Writing Cards Set 6

26. The Constitution is the highest law of the land.

_____

_____

27. Americans have freedom of speech.

_____

_____

28. The Bill of Rights gives us freedom.

_____

_____

29. U.S. citizens can vote in elections.

_____

_____

30. Citizens have the right to vote.

_____

_____

Test Hint #6

If you do not answer a question quickly, the examiner might think that you don't know the answer. But maybe you need a little more time to think.

Here are some words that tell an examiner that you are still thinking of the answer:

- let's see . . .
- let me think . . .
- let me see . . .

Examiner:

Applicant:

What is the Constitution?

Uh . . . let's see . . . It's the highest law.

You can also repeat some words from the question.
Here's an example:

What is the Bill of Rights?

The Bill of Rights? . . . It's the first ten amendments to the Constitution.

You can use both ways together.

When was the Constitution written?

The Constitution? . . . Uh . . . let me see . . . in 1787.

Try the Test

Mark the answer box with the best answer for each question.

1. Where does freedom of speech come from?
   A. the Declaration of Independence
   B. the Bill of Rights
   C. the Emancipation Proclamation
   D. the Magna Carta

2. How many amendments are there to the Constitution?
   A. 12
   B. 10
   C. 50
   D. 27

3. What is the Constitution?
   A. the supreme law of the land
   B. a paper that freed the slaves
   C. the first part of the Declaration of Independence
   D. a letter to the King of England

4. What are the first 10 amendments to the Constitution called?
   A. the Mayflower
   B. the Bill of Rights
   C. the Preamble
   D. the Declaration of Independence

5. How many branches are there in our government?
   A. two
   B. three
   C. four
   D. five

6. Why is the Bill of Rights important?
   A. It gives freedom to people in Canada.
   B. It gives money to disabled Americans.
   C. It gives rights to all people in the U.S.
   D. It gives rights to people in neighboring countries.

1. Ⓐ Ⓑ Ⓒ Ⓓ	4. Ⓐ Ⓑ Ⓒ Ⓓ
2. Ⓐ Ⓑ Ⓒ Ⓓ	5. Ⓐ Ⓑ Ⓒ Ⓓ
3. Ⓐ Ⓑ Ⓒ Ⓓ	6. Ⓐ Ⓑ Ⓒ Ⓓ

Writing Test 📼

26. _____

27. _____

28. _____

29. _____

30. _____

7. The Executive Branch

Legislative Branch

Judicial Branch

The president is the head of the **executive branch.**

The **official** home of the president is the **White House.**
The White House is located in Washington, D.C.

Spelling

White House _____

home _____

What Does It Mean?

official = for his job

located = in a place

Presidents of the United States

Carter, James E.
1977-1981

Reagan, Ronald W.
1981-1985
1985-1989

Bush, George H.
1989-1993

Clinton, William J.
1993- 1997
1997- 2001

Americans elect the president for four years at a time.

A president can be elected two times.

A president can serve two **terms.**

Spelling	What Does It Mean?
term _____	term = years a leader is elected for
serve _____	serve = be an elected leader
years _____	

Election Day is in November.

NOVEMBER						
S	M	T	W	T	F	S
	1	2	3	4	5	6
7	8	9	10	11	12	13
14	15	16	17	18	19	20
21	22	23	24	25	26	27
28	29	30				

VOTE

Elections for president are in November.

But the new president does not start his job until January.

The new president is **inaugurated** in January.

Spelling

November _____

January _____

does _____

What Does It Mean?

inaugurated = officially becomes president

There are some **requirements** for a person who wants to be president.

The person must be 35 years old and a **natural-born citizen.**

Spelling	What Does It Mean?
born _____	requirements = what a person needs
person _____	natural-born citizen = born in the U.S.

The **vice president** helps the president.

If the president dies, the vice president becomes the new president.

Who is the current vice president? _____

Spelling

vice president _____

new _____

The president is **commander in chief** of the U.S. **military.**
The president leads the U.S. armed forces.

What Does It Mean?

military = army, navy, air force, marines

The president has a special group of people who advise him.

They help him run the government.

This group is called the **Cabinet.**

What Does It Mean?

advise = help

run = make something work

The executive branch is the president, the Cabinet, and the
   departments under them.
The executive branch makes the U.S. government run.

Spelling	**What Does It Mean?**
under _____	departments = offices
run _____	

What Does It Mean?

1. advise

2. military

3. Cabinet

4. natural-born citizen

5. official

6. the White House

7. inaugurated

- born in the U.S.

- for the government

- The president lives here.

- army, navy, air force, and marines

- help

- group of people who help the president

- officially becomes president

Yes or No?

yes   no   1. The Cabinet advises the president.

yes   no   2. A person who is 25 years old can be president.

yes   no   3. The president and his wife are the executive branch.

yes   no   4. The president's official home is the White House.

yes   no   5. Americans elect a president every 4 years.

yes   no   6. A president can serve for 4 terms of office.

yes   no   7. If the president dies, the vice president becomes the new president.

yes   no   8. The vice president is commander in chief of the U.S. military.

yes   no   9. A president can be elected three times.

yes   no   10. A person born in Canada can be elected president.

Spelling

A. Fill in the missing letters for words in this lesson.

1. ye__rs
2. __ovemb__r
3. ser__e
4. bo__n
5. vic__ presi__ent
6. W__ite Ho__se

B. Now use the same words to fill in the blanks.

1. A president can _____ for two terms.

2. We elect a president for four _____.

3. We elect a president in _____.

4. The _____ _____ is the official home of the president.

5. The _____ _____ becomes the new president if the president dies.

6. The president must be a natural-_____ citizen.

Say the Answer

1. Who is the vice president of the U.S. today?

2. Who elects the president of the U.S.?

3. What is the executive branch of the government?

4. How many terms can a president serve?

5. In what month do we vote for president?

6. Where is the White House located?

7. In what month is the new president inaugurated?

8. What are some requirements for a person to become president?

Writing Cards Set 7

31. Election Day is in November.

_____

_____

32. The vice president helps the president.

_____

_____

33. A president can serve two terms.

_____

_____

34. The president serves for four years.

_____

_____

35. The president lives in the White House.

_____

_____

Test Hint #7

Some questions almost sound the same.

Who was the first president of the United States?
Who is the president of the United States?

Be careful! The answers are different. If you're not sure, ask the examiner to repeat the question. Or check to make sure that you heard the question right. For example:

Examiner:

Applicant:

Who was the first president?   The president today?

No. The first president.

Here are more questions that sound alike:
  • Who is the commander in chief of the U.S. military?
  • Who was the first commander in chief of the U.S. military?

Who is the commander in chief   You mean today?
of the U.S. military?

Yes, who is the commander in
chief right now?

Try the Test

Mark the answer box with the best answer for each question.

1. Which branch of government does the president serve in?
   A. the legislative branch
   B. the executive branch
   C. the judicial branch
   D. He doesn't serve in any branch.

2. What is the job of the executive branch?
   A. to make sure the Cabinet works hard
   B. to make the U.S. government run
   C. to make the laws for the country
   D. to live in the White House

3. What is the name of the president's official home?
   A. the Washington Monument
   B. Independence Hall
   C. the Capitol
   D. the White House

4. For how long do we elect the president?
   A. six years
   B. two years
   C. four years
   D. nine years

5. What special group advises the president?
   A. the military
   B. the FBI
   C. the legislative branch
   D. the Cabinet

6. Which of these people can be elected president?
   A. a 35-year-old woman born in New York
   B. a 69-year-old man born in Canada
   C. a 40-year-old woman born in Mexico
   D. a 30-year-old man born in Washington, D.C.

```
1. Ⓐ Ⓑ Ⓒ Ⓓ    4. Ⓐ Ⓑ Ⓒ Ⓓ
2. Ⓐ Ⓑ Ⓒ Ⓓ    5. Ⓐ Ⓑ Ⓒ Ⓓ
3. Ⓐ Ⓑ Ⓒ Ⓓ    6. Ⓐ Ⓑ Ⓒ Ⓓ
```

Writing Test

31. _____

32. _____

33. _____

34. _____

35. _____

8. The Legislative Branch

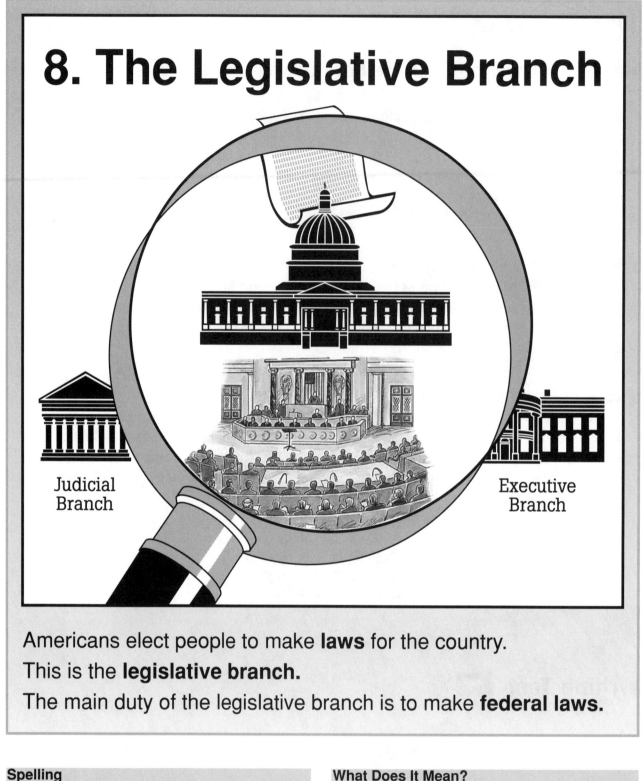

Judicial Branch

Executive Branch

Americans elect people to make **laws** for the country.

This is the **legislative branch.**

The main duty of the legislative branch is to make **federal laws.**

Spelling

make _____

What Does It Mean?

duty = job, work

federal = for the whole U.S.

Another name for the legislative branch is **Congress.**
Congress meets in a building called the **Capitol.**
The Capitol is in Washington, D.C.

Spelling	**What Does It Mean?**

Congress _____   meets = works together

Capitol _____

meets _____

Judicial Branch

House of Representatives

Senate

Executive Branch

There are two parts of Congress: the **Senate** and the **House of Representatives.**

These are the two **houses** of Congress.

Spelling	What Does It Mean?
Senate _____	house of Congress = part of Congress
two _____	
house _____	

United States Senators

Michigan
Debbie Stabenow
2001-

New Mexico
Pete Domenici
1973-1979
1979-1985
1985-1991
1991-1997
1997-

Colorado
Ben Nighthorse Campbell
1993-1999
1999-

Hawaii
Daniel K. Inouye
1963-1969
1969-1975
1975-1981
1981-1987
1987-1993
1993-1999
1999-

California
Barbara Boxer
1993-1999
1999-

Senators work in the Senate.

Americans elect senators for six-year terms.

Voters can re-elect a senator as many times as they want.

There is no limit.

Spelling

senators _____

six _____

What Does It Mean?

re-elect = elect again

limit = highest number possible

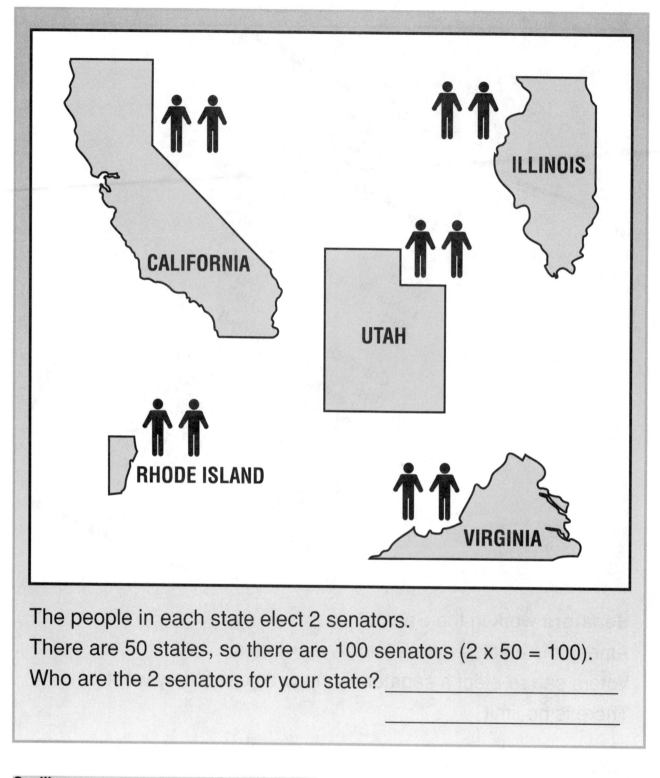

The people in each state elect 2 senators.

There are 50 states, so there are 100 senators (2 x 50 = 100).

Who are the 2 senators for your state? _____

_____

Spelling

each _____

United States Representatives

Tennessee
Bob Clement
1989-1991
1991-1993
1993-1995
1995-1997
1997-1999
1999-2001
2001-

Iowa
James A. Leach
1977-1979
1979-1981
1981-1983
1983-1985
1985-1987
1987-1989
1989-1991
1991-1993
1993-1995
1995-1997
1997-1999
1999-2001
2001-

Wisconsin
Tammy Baldwin
1999-2001
2001-

California
Loretta Sanchez
1997-1999
1999-2001
2001-

Texas
Sheila Jackson Lee
1995-1997
1997-1999
1999-2001
2001-

Representatives work in the House of Representatives.

Americans elect representatives for two-year terms.

Voters can re-elect a representative as many times as they want.

There is no limit.

Spelling

want _____

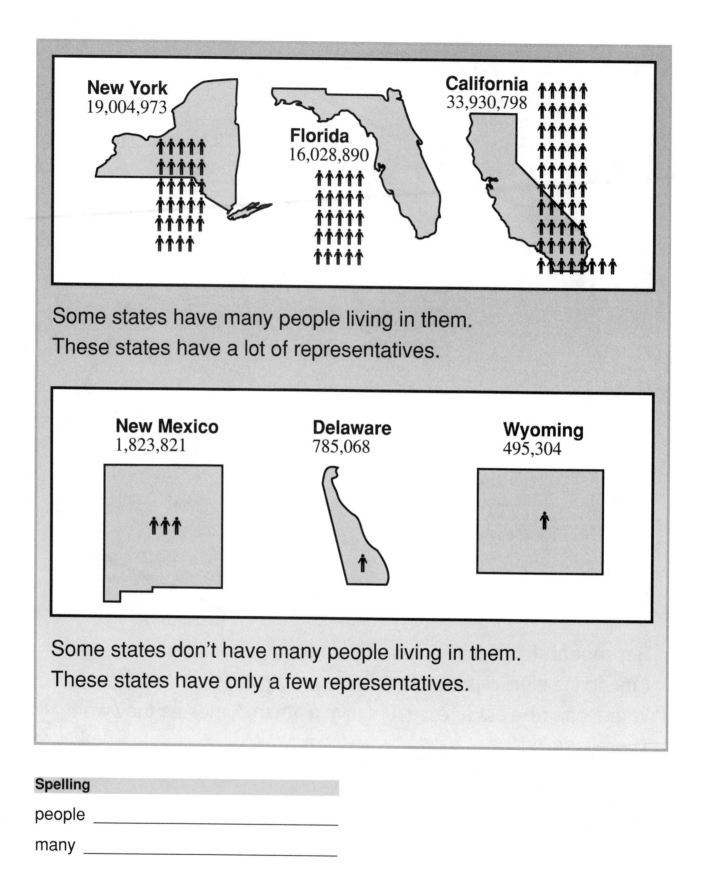

New York
19,004,973

Florida
16,028,890

California
33,930,798

Some states have many people living in them.
These states have a lot of representatives.

New Mexico
1,823,821

Delaware
785,068

Wyoming
495,304

Some states don't have many people living in them.
These states have only a few representatives.

Spelling

people _____

many _____

The number of representatives for a state depends on the
number of people who live in the state.

There are 435 voting members in the House of Representatives.

Spelling

live _____

A representative is sometimes called a **congressman** or **congresswoman.**

What is the name of your representative? _____

The leader of the House of Representatives is called the Speaker. If the president and vice president both die, the **Speaker of the House** becomes the new president.

An idea for a new law is called a bill.

The people in Congress vote on bills. If Congress **passes** the bill, the bill goes to the president.

If the president **signs the bill,** it becomes a law.

What Does It Mean?

pass = vote to accept

bill = plan for a new law

Sometimes the president does not agree with Congress. Sometimes he does not sign the bill. This is called a **veto.** If a president vetoes a bill, it usually does not become a law.

What Does It Mean?

veto = say "no" to a bill

Congress **has the power** to **declare war.**
Only Congress can decide whether the U.S. will fight a war.

Spelling	**What Does It Mean?**
has _____	has the power = can
only _____	declare = decide something important

What Does It Mean?

1. Congress
2. the Capitol
3. duty
4. meets
5. the House of Representatives
6. the Senate

- works together
- group of 100 lawmakers
- group of 435 lawmakers
- the Senate and the House of Representatives
- Congress meets here.
- job

Yes or No?

yes   no   1. Congress has the power to declare war.

yes   no   2. Congress has two houses, or parts.

yes   no   3. Another name for Congress is the executive branch.

yes   no   4. The main duty of the legislative branch is to elect the president.

yes   no   5. Congress meets in the White House.

yes   no   6. The Senate and the House of Representatives make up the legislative branch.

yes   no   7. Representatives are elected for 6 years.

yes   no   8. Congress meets in the Capitol.

yes   no   9. The main duty of Congress is to make the country's laws.

yes   no   10. There are 50 senators, one for each state.

Spelling

A. Fill in the missing letters for words in this lesson.

1. Capito__
2. Cong__ess
3. liv__

4. e__ch
5. m__kes
6. t__o

7. mee__s
8. peopl__
9. ho__se

10. sen__tors
11. Sena__e

B. Now use the same words to fill in the blanks.

1. There are two senators for _____ state.

2. Representatives are elected by the _____ .

3. Congress _____ the laws.

4. Congress _____ in the _____ .

5. There are two houses, or parts, of _____ .

6. States with many _____ have many representatives.

Say the Answer

1. What are the two houses of Congress?
2. Who elects Congress?
3. Can you name the two senators from your state?
4. Who becomes president of the U.S. if both the president and the vice president die?
5. Who signs bills into law?
6. What is the U.S. Capitol?
7. How many times can a senator be re-elected?
8. How many times can a congressman be re-elected?

Writing Cards Set 8

36. Each state has two senators.

_____

_____

37. Congress makes the laws.

_____

_____

38. Congress meets in the Capitol.

_____

_____

39. There are two houses of Congress.

_____

_____

40. Senators are elected by the people.

_____

_____

Test Hint #8

If you don't know what kind of answer the examiner wants, ask a question to make it more clear. Here are some examples.

Examiner:

Applicant:

For how long do we elect each representative?

For how many <u>years</u>?

How many senators are there in Congress?

What <u>number</u>?

Who was the main writer of the Declaration of Independence?

Who <u>wrote</u> it?

What is the minimum voting age?

How <u>old</u>?

When was the Declaration of Independence adopted?

What <u>year</u>?

Try the Test

Mark the answer box with the best answer for each question.

1. Who makes federal laws in the U.S.?
   A. the president
   B. Congress
   C. the armed forces
   D. governors

2. What is the legislative branch of our government?
   A. the White House
   B. the Cabinet
   C. Congress
   D. the Capitol

3. Where does Congress meet?
   A. the Capitol
   B. the White House
   C. Independence Hall
   D. the legislative branch

4. For how long do we elect each senator?
   A. four years
   B. six years
   C. two years
   D. five years

5. What group has the power to declare war?
   A. the American voters
   B. the president and vice president
   C. Congress
   D. the Cabinet

6. How many senators are there in Congress?
   A. 435
   B. 50
   C. 27
   D. 100

1. Ⓐ Ⓑ Ⓒ Ⓓ   4. Ⓐ Ⓑ Ⓒ Ⓓ
2. Ⓐ Ⓑ Ⓒ Ⓓ   5. Ⓐ Ⓑ Ⓒ Ⓓ
3. Ⓐ Ⓑ Ⓒ Ⓓ   6. Ⓐ Ⓑ Ⓒ Ⓓ

Writing Test

36. _____

37. _____

38. _____

39. _____

40. _____

9. The Judicial Branch

There are many kinds of courts in the U.S.
For example, there are **federal courts** and state courts.

Spelling

court _____

many _____

What Does It Mean?

federal = for the whole U.S.

The highest U.S. court is the **Supreme Court.**
It meets in Washington, D.C.

Spelling

Washington,
D.C. _____

The Supreme Court and other federal courts are the **judicial branch.**

Spelling

supreme _____

are _____

other _____

The duties of the judicial branch are to **interpret and explain the laws.**

To interpret a law means to explain how it works in everyday life.

Spelling	What Does It Mean?
works _____	interpret = explain
how _____	

The Supreme Court decides whether laws are **constitutional** or **unconstitutional.**

If a law is unconstitutional, it must be changed.

Spelling	What Does It Mean?
must _____	constitutional = agrees with the Constitution unconstitutional = doesn't agree with the Constitution

There are nine **justices** on the Supreme Court.

The leader of the Supreme Court is the **Chief Justice.**

Who is the current Chief Justice of the Supreme Court? _____

Spelling

nine _____

What Does It Mean?

justice = judge =

Justices are not elected.
The president picks them.
The president **nominates** Supreme Court justices.

What Does It Mean?

nominates = picks

What Does It Mean?

1. the Supreme Court

2. interprets

3. Chief Justice

4. constitutional

5. unconstitutional

6. federal

7. nominates

- doesn't agree with the Constitution

- for the whole U.S.

- the highest court in the U.S.

- explains

- picks

- agrees with the Constitution

- leader of the Supreme Court

Yes or No?

yes   no   1. The Supreme Court is the highest U.S. court.

yes   no   2. The work of the judicial branch is to make laws.

yes   no   3. If a law is unconstitutional, it must be changed.

yes   no   4. There are five justices on the Supreme Court.

yes   no   5. Supreme Court justices are elected by the people.

yes   no   6. The president nominates the justices for the Supreme Court.

yes   no   7. The Supreme Court meets in New York City.

yes   no   8. The highest federal court is the Supreme Court.

yes   no   9. The judicial branch interprets the laws of the U.S.

yes   no   10. There is only one kind of court in the U.S.

yes   no   11. The leader of the Supreme Court is the Chief Justice.

Spelling

A. Fill in the missing letters for words in this lesson.

1. m__st   4. W__shing__on, D.C.
2. Supre__e Cour__   5. w__rk
3. m__ny   6. ni__e

B. Now use the same words to fill in the blanks.

1. The highest U.S. court is the _____ _____ .

2. The _____ of the Supreme Court is to interpret laws.

3. The Supreme Court meets in _____ _____ .

4. A law that is unconstitutional _____ be changed.

5. There are _____ justices on the Supreme Court.

Say the Answer

1. Who is the Chief Justice of the Supreme Court?
2. What is the judicial branch of our government?
3. Who selects the Supreme Court justices?
4. What are the duties of the Supreme Court?
5. How many Supreme Court justices are there?

Writing Cards Set 9

41. The Supreme Court is in Washington, D.C.

_____

_____

42. Washington, D.C., is the U.S. capital.

_____

_____

43. We must honor our country's flag.

_____

_____

44. The White House is in Washington, D.C.

_____

_____

45. I want to be an American citizen.

_____

_____

Test Hint #9

Sometimes it's hard to remember new words. For example:

Examiner:

Applicant:

What is the duty of the Supreme Court?

To in . . . in . . . I can't remember the word. It means telling how a law works in everyday life.

Do you mean interpret?

Yes. To interpret the laws.

Here is another example:

What do we call the people who serve on the Supreme Court?

They're called . . . I can't remember the word. It sounds like judge.

Maybe you're thinking of justice.

Yes. They're called justices.

If you can't remember an important word, try to explain it instead. This way you can show the examiner you understand the questions.

Try the Test

Mark the answer box with the best answer for each question.

1. How many Supreme Court justices are there?
   A. 9
   B. 50
   C. 4
   D. 27

2. What are the duties of the Supreme Court?
   A. to enforce the laws
   B. to make the laws
   C. to interpret and explain the laws
   D. to see that the laws are carried out

3. Who serves on the Supreme Court?
   A. senators
   B. justices
   C. representatives
   D. Cabinet members

4. What is the highest court in the U.S.?
   A. district court
   B. circuit court
   C. the Superior Court
   D. the Supreme Court

5. The Supreme Court and other federal courts make up which branch of government?
   A. the judicial branch
   B. the presidential branch
   C. the executive branch
   D. the legislative branch

6. Who nominates judges for the Supreme Court?
   A. Congress
   B. the president
   C. the Chief Justice

1. Ⓐ Ⓑ Ⓒ Ⓓ   4. Ⓐ Ⓑ Ⓒ Ⓓ
2. Ⓐ Ⓑ Ⓒ Ⓓ   5. Ⓐ Ⓑ Ⓒ Ⓓ
3. Ⓐ Ⓑ Ⓒ Ⓓ   6. Ⓐ Ⓑ Ⓒ Ⓓ

Writing Test

41. _____

42. _____

43. _____

44. _____

45. _____

Government Review

Match

Find the words that go with the pictures.
Copy the words on the lines.

a justice

the Capitol

1. _____

4. _____

the Supreme Court

the U.S. military

Congress

2. _____

5. _____

the White House

3. _____

6. _____

Which Branch Are They In?

Put the government leaders in the right branch.

✓president	representatives	justices
senators	vice president	Cabinet

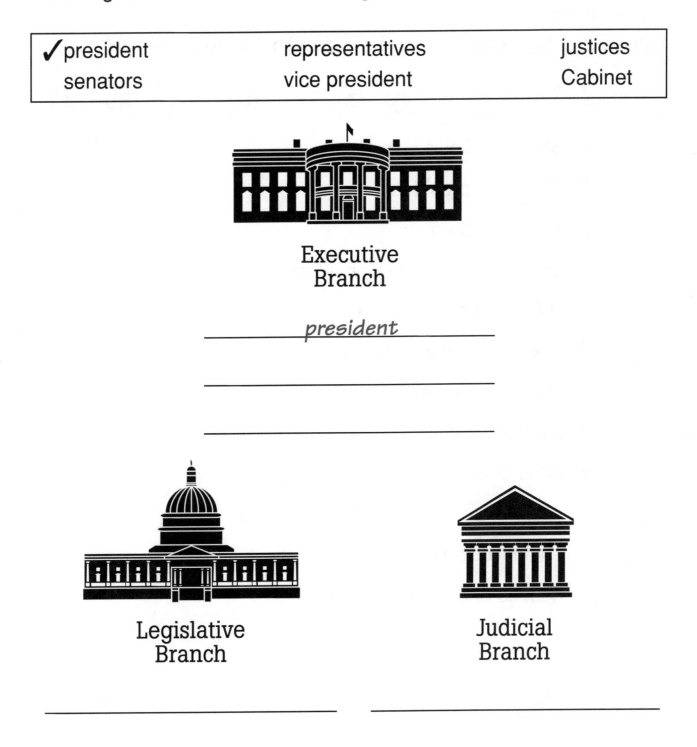

Executive Branch

_____ *president* _____

_____

_____

Legislative Branch

Judicial Branch

_____   _____

_____

Important Numbers

Here are some important numbers in American history and government.

Can you remember which numbers go with the words below?

| 50 | 2 | 13 | 9 | 4 | 6 | 27 | 2 | 100 | 435 | 10 | 13 |

_9_ 1. Supreme Court justices

_____ 2. years in a president's term

_____ 3. stripes on the flag

_____ 4. amendments to the Constitution

_____ 5. U.S. senators

_____ 6. years a senator is elected for

_____ 7. U.S. representatives

_____ 8. states in the U.S.

_____ 9. amendments in the Bill of Rights

_____ 10. years a representative is elected for

_____ 11. original colonies

_____ 12. houses of Congress

Which Branch Is It?

Write **L** for the legislative branch.
Write **E** for the executive branch.
Write **J** for the judicial branch.

_J_   1. interprets the laws

_____   2. makes the laws

_____   3. nine justices

_____   4. the Senate and the House of Representatives

_____   5. the president, the vice president, and the Cabinet

_____   6. nominated by the president

_____   7. has the power to declare war

_____   8. 100 senators and 435 representatives

_____   9. decides whether a law is constitutional

_____   10. can sign a bill into law

_____   11. Congress

_____   12. meets in the Capitol

_____   13. the Supreme Court

_____   14. makes the U.S. government run

Which Is It?

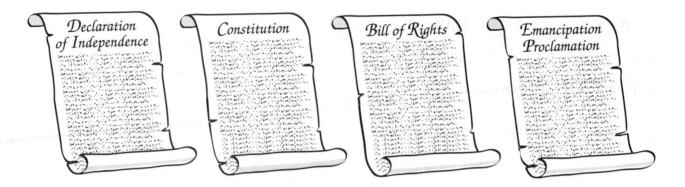

Write **D** for the Declaration of Independence.
Write **C** for the Constitution.
Write **B** for the Bill of Rights.
Write **E** for the Emancipation Proclamation.

_D_ 1. Thomas Jefferson wrote this.

_____ 2. Abraham Lincoln signed it.

_____ 3. It gives all Americans the right to free speech.

_____ 4. The 13 colonies decided they would be independent from England.

_____ 5. It freed slaves.

_____ 6. It was written in the 1860s.

_____ 7. It's the supreme law of the land.

_____ 8. It has 27 amendments.

_____ 9. It was signed on July 4, 1776.

_____ 10. It's the first 10 amendments to the Constitution.

_____ 11. It says all people are created equal.

Government Test A

Mark the answer box with the best answer for each question.

1. What is the executive branch?
   A. the president, the Cabinet, and departments under them
   B. 9 Supreme Court justices
   C. senators and representatives
   D. mayors and governors

2. What special group advises the president?
   A. the army
   B. the Supreme Court
   C. the Senate
   D. the Cabinet

3. What is the Bill of Rights?
   A. the introduction to the Declaration of Independence
   B. the paper that abolished slavery
   C. the first 10 amendments to the Constitution
   D. the money it costs to run the government

4. What is an amendment?
   A. a letter to the King of England
   B. a judge on the Supreme Court
   C. a change to the U.S. flag
   D. a change to the Constitution

5. What is the judicial branch?
   A. the Senate
   B. Congress
   C. the Supreme Court and other federal courts
   D. the president and the Cabinet

6. Which branch of government interprets the laws of the U.S.?
   A. the judicial branch
   B. the legislative branch
   C. the executive branch
   D. Congress

7. The House of Representatives and the Senate make up which branch of government?
   A. the legislative branch
   B. the executive branch
   C. the judicial branch
   D. the Cabinet

8. What does the legislative branch do?
   A. explains the laws
   B. protests unfair laws
   C. runs the government
   D. makes the laws

1. Ⓐ Ⓑ Ⓒ Ⓓ   5. Ⓐ Ⓑ Ⓒ Ⓓ
2. Ⓐ Ⓑ Ⓒ Ⓓ   6. Ⓐ Ⓑ Ⓒ Ⓓ
3. Ⓐ Ⓑ Ⓒ Ⓓ   7. Ⓐ Ⓑ Ⓒ Ⓓ
4. Ⓐ Ⓑ Ⓒ Ⓓ   8. Ⓐ Ⓑ Ⓒ Ⓓ

Writing Test 📼

A. _____

B. _____

Government Test B

Mark the circle next to the best answer for each question.

1. What does the Cabinet do?
   - ◯ A. helps the president
   - ◯ B. makes laws
   - ◯ C. helps the Supreme Court
   - ◯ D. interprets laws

2. Which government officials must be native-born citizens?
   - ◯ A. senators
   - ◯ B. governors
   - ◯ C. court justices
   - ◯ D. presidents

3. Which group does **not** have rights under the Constitution?
   - ◯ A. people who live in England
   - ◯ B. U.S. citizens
   - ◯ C. people who live in the U.S.
   - ◯ D. non-citizens in the U.S.

4. Which group of government leaders is nominated by the president?
   - ◯ A. senators
   - ◯ B. representatives
   - ◯ C. Supreme Court justices
   - ◯ D. governors

5. Which branch of government does the Supreme Court belong to?
   - ◯ A. the judicial branch
   - ◯ B. the executive branch
   - ◯ C. the legislative branch
   - ◯ D. the military branch

6. What does the number of representatives for each state depend on?
   - ◯ A. how much land the state has
   - ◯ B. how close it is to Washington, D.C.
   - ◯ C. how many people live in the state
   - ◯ D. when the state joined the Union

7. For how long do we elect a representative?
   - ◯ A. 4 years
   - ◯ B. 2 years
   - ◯ C. 6 years
   - ◯ D. There is no limit.

8. How many senators are elected by each state?
   - ◯ A. It depends on how many people live there.
   - ◯ B. 5
   - ◯ C. 2
   - ◯ D. 100

9. What is the supreme law of the United States?
   - ◯ A. the Emancipation Proclamation
   - ◯ B. the Constitution
   - ◯ C. the Declaration of Independence
   - ◯ D. the Magna Carta

10. What do we call changes to the Constitution?
    - ◯ A. amendments
    - ◯ B. preambles
    - ◯ C. arbitrations
    - ◯ D. bills

Writing Test 📼

A. _____

B. _____

Test Hint for Current Leaders

Who is the head of your local government?

Every city has a mayor.

If you live in a city, you need to find out the name of your city's mayor.

Many towns have a group called a select board or a town council.

Some towns have a town manager.

If you live in a town, you need to find out what kind of leader your town has. You need to know the name of this leader.

Who can you ask?

- a teacher
- a friend
- a librarian
- a town or city worker

CURRENT LEADERS

- The **president** of the U.S. today is _____ _____.
- The **vice president** of the U.S. is _____ _____.
- The **Chief Justice** of the Supreme Court is
  _____ _____.

- The name of my **state** is _____.
- The 2 **senators** for my state are _____ _____
  and _____ _____.
- The name of my **congressman** or **congresswoman** is
  _____ _____.

- The **capital** of my state is _____.

- The **governor** of my state is _____ _____.

- The name of my **city** or **town** is _____.

- The **leader** of my city or town is _____ _____.

Review Test 1

Mark the circle next to the best answer for each question.

1. Who did the U.S. fight against in World War I?
   - ○ A. France
   - ○ B. Germany
   - ○ C. England
   - ○ D. Russia

2. In what month is a new president inaugurated?
   - ○ A. October
   - ○ B. July
   - ○ C. January
   - ○ D. November

3. Who was Abraham Lincoln?
   - ○ A. the president during World War II
   - ○ B. the president during the Civil War
   - ○ C. the King of England
   - ○ D. the first president of the United States

4. Who was an important civil rights leader in the 1960s?
   - ○ A. Thomas Jefferson
   - ○ B. George Washington
   - ○ C. Susan B. Anthony
   - ○ D. Martin Luther King Jr.

5. Who came to America for religious freedom?
   - ○ A. the Pilgrims
   - ○ B. the slaves
   - ○ C. the Native Americans
   - ○ D. Christopher Columbus

6. Who becomes our president if the president dies?
   - ○ A. the Chief Justice of the Supreme Court
   - ○ B. the Speaker of the House of Representatives
   - ○ C. the vice president
   - ○ D. the mayor of Washington, D.C.

7. The president, the Cabinet, and the departments under them make up which branch of government?
   - ○ A. the executive branch
   - ○ B. the judicial branch
   - ○ C. the legislative branch
   - ○ D. the armed forces branch

8. What is the head executive of a state called?
   - ○ A. president
   - ○ B. mayor
   - ○ C. governor
   - ○ D. senator

9. Who meets in the U.S. Capitol building?
   - ○ A. the president and his Cabinet
   - ○ B. the Supreme Court
   - ○ C. Congress
   - ○ D. the Conference of Governors

10. How old must a person be to run for president of the U.S.?
    - ○ A. 18 years old
    - ○ B. 25 years old
    - ○ C. 45 years old
    - ○ D. 35 years old

11. What is another name for the legislative branch?
    - ○ A. the Capitol
    - ○ B. the Congress
    - ○ C. the Supreme Court
    - ○ D. the Union

12. Who chooses senators and representatives?
    - ○ A. the president
    - ○ B. the Supreme Court
    - ○ C. the people who vote in elections
    - ○ D. the governors of the 50 states

13. Where does a justice serve?
    - ○ A. in the Supreme Court
    - ○ B. in the Senate
    - ○ C. in a state capital
    - ○ D. in the White House

14. What war did the U.S. fight in the 1860s?
    - ○ A. the Revolutionary War
    - ○ B. the Civil War
    - ○ C. the Korean War
    - ○ D. World War II

15. What army won the Civil War?
    - ○ A. the Republican Army
    - ○ B. the Civil Army
    - ○ C. the Union Army
    - ○ D. the Confederate Army

16. What country did the American colonists fight against in the Revolutionary War?
    - ○ A. Germany
    - ○ B. Vietnam
    - ○ C. England
    - ○ D. Mexico

17. Who came to America on a ship called the Mayflower?
    - ○ A. the Native Americans
    - ○ B. the Pilgrims
    - ○ C. the slaves
    - ○ D. the Confederate Army

18. Who is commander in chief of the U.S. military?
    - ○ A. the Speaker of the House of Representatives
    - ○ B. the president
    - ○ C. the Chief Justice of the Supreme Court
    - ○ D. the secretary of state

19. When did Christopher Columbus come to America?
    - ○ A. in 1492
    - ○ B. in 1776
    - ○ C. in 1860
    - ○ D. in 1960

20. Who was the leader of the Colonial Army during the Revolutionary War?
    - ○ A. Thomas Jefferson
    - ○ B. George Washington
    - ○ C. the King of England
    - ○ D. Ben Franklin

Writing Test 🔲

A. _____

B. _____

The sentences for the Writing Test are on the audio recording and on page 192.

Review Test 2

Mark the circle next to the best answer for each question.

1. The U.S. fought against Germany and Japan in which war?
   - ○ A. the Civil War
   - ○ B. the Revolutionary War
   - ○ C. the Korean War
   - ○ D. World War II

2. When did the 13 colonies become the United States of America?
   - ○ A. July 4, 1776
   - ○ B. June 6, 1676
   - ○ C. July 4, 1860
   - ○ D. June 24, 1492

3. Which important paper says, "All men are created equal"?
   - ○ A. the Emancipation Proclamation
   - ○ B. the Constitution
   - ○ C. the Declaration of Independence
   - ○ D. the Bill of Rights

4. What do the stars on the U.S. flag stand for?
   - ○ A. the original 13 colonies
   - ○ B. the 50 states
   - ○ C. the members of the Supreme Court
   - ○ D. the first Native American nations

5. What are the names of the two main political parties?
   - ○ A. the Senate and the House of Representatives
   - ○ B. the Union Party and the Confederate Party
   - ○ C. the Atlantic Party and the Pacific Party
   - ○ D. the Republican Party and the Democratic Party

6. What holiday did the Pilgrims celebrate for the first time?
   - ○ A. Presidents' Day
   - ○ B. Independence Day
   - ○ C. Thanksgiving
   - ○ D. Columbus Day

7. What do the stripes on the U.S. flag stand for?
   - ○ A. the original 13 states
   - ○ B. the first 13 settlements
   - ○ C. the first 13 presidents
   - ○ D. the 13 leaders of the American Revolution

8. Who wrote "The Star-Spangled Banner"?
   - ○ A. Patrick Henry
   - ○ B. Francis Scott Key
   - ○ C. Thomas Jefferson
   - ○ D. Christopher Columbus

9. Why is Thomas Jefferson famous?
   - ○ A. He wrote the Declaration of Independence.
   - ○ B. He was the first president.
   - ○ C. He freed the slaves.
   - ○ D. He was the first English colonist to come to America.

10. The Bill of Rights gives Americans the right to
   - ○ A. travel to any country
   - ○ B. own slaves
   - ○ C. speak freely
   - ○ D. make their own currency

11. Which amendments guarantee voting rights?
  ○ A. 1, 2, and 3
  ○ B. 10, 14, and 18
  ○ C. 14, 15, and 19
  ○ D. 21, 23, and 27

12. What is Congress?
  ○ A. the executive branch
  ○ B. the Supreme Court
  ○ C. the legislative branch
  ○ D. the Cabinet

13. How many voting members are in the House of Representatives?
  ○ A. 345
  ○ B. 100
  ○ C. 50
  ○ D. 435

14. What is the highest law of the United States?
  ○ A. the constitution of each state
  ○ B. the U.S. Constitution
  ○ C. the Congressional Record
  ○ D. local government ordinances

15. Who meets in the Capitol in Washington, D.C.?
  ○ A. the Supreme Court
  ○ B. the president and the vice president
  ○ C. the Cabinet
  ○ D. Congress

16. What is the name of the president's official home?
  ○ A. the Capitol
  ○ B. the Washington Monument
  ○ C. Camp David
  ○ D. the White House

17. Where does freedom of speech come from?
  ○ A. the Bill of Rights
  ○ B. the Declaration of Independence
  ○ C. the Emancipation Proclamation
  ○ D. the Mayflower Compact

18. How many terms can a president serve?
  ○ A. two
  ○ B. four
  ○ C. six
  ○ D. no set number of terms

19. Which branch makes the U.S. government run?
  ○ A. the Supreme Court
  ○ B. the executive branch
  ○ C. the judicial branch
  ○ D. the legislative branch

20. What happened on July 4, 1776?
  ○ A. Abraham Lincoln freed the slaves.
  ○ B. Christopher Columbus came to America.
  ○ C. The Pilgrims started the first American colony.
  ○ D. The Declaration of Independence was signed.

Writing Test 🎞

A. _____

B. _____

The sentences for the Writing Test are on the audio recording and on page 192.

Sentences for Writing Practice

- The Statue of Liberty is in New York harbor.

- The Pilgrims came to America for freedom.

- Americans have freedom of religion.

- There are 13 stripes on the U.S. flag.

- The U.S. government has three branches.

- The president signs bills into law.

- The stars on the flag stand for the 50 states.

- The leader of a state is the governor.

- The United States grew after the Civil War.

- Martin Luther King Jr. was a civil rights leader.

- George Washington was the father of our country.

- The Constitution is the supreme law of the land.

- Congress works in the Capitol.

- There are nine justices on the Supreme Court.

- Congress makes laws for the country.

- The Bill of Rights gives Americans freedom of speech.

- Alaska and Hawaii joined the Union in 1959.

- The Cabinet advises the president.

- The White House is the home of the president.

- You must be 18 years old to vote.

- I want to be a citizen of the United States.

- I am studying English.

- Washington, D.C., is the capital of the United States.

- Only U.S. citizens can vote.

Citizenship Word List

Answer Key

1. Welcome to the United States

Match (page 18)

1. United States
2. city
3. Statue of Liberty
4. stars
5. flag
6. states

What Does It Mean? (page 19)

1. president = head executive of the U.S.
2. governor = leader of a state
3. capital = The government is here.
4. mayor = leader of a city
5. democracy = People choose their leaders.
6. national = of our country
7. anthem = song

Yes or No? (page 19)

1. no
2. yes
3. no
4. no
5. yes
6. yes
7. yes
8. no
9. yes
10. yes
11. no
12. yes

Spelling (page 20)

A. 1. blue
   2. capital
   3. colors
   4. elections
   5. flag
   6. every
   7. red
   8. stars
   9. states
   10. there
   11. white
   12. city

B. 1. The U.S. has 50 states.
   2. Red, white, and blue are the colors of the flag.
   3. We choose leaders by voting in elections.
   4. There are 50 stars on the U.S. flag.
   5. Washington, D.C., is the capital of the U.S.

Say the Answer (page 20)

1. The answer depends on where you live.
2. The answer depends on where you live.
3. The answer depends on where you live.
4. The answer will change with time.
5. Francis Scott Key
6. red and white
7. red, white, and blue
8. white

Try the Test (page 25)

1. B
2. C
3. B
4. D
5. C
6. D

Writing Test (page 25)

1. The stars on the flag are white.
2. The U.S. flag has 50 stars.
3. The colors of the flag are red, white, and blue.
4. There are 50 states in the U.S.
5. The capital of the U.S. is Washington, D.C.

2. America's Early History

Match (page 34)

1. Pilgrims
2. ship
3. the 13 colonies
4. Christopher Columbus
5. England
6. Native Americans

What Does It Mean? (page 35)

1. coast = land next to the sea
2. the Mayflower = the Pilgrims' ship
3. colonies = places where people start new homes
4. religious = the way people think about God
5. celebrate = get together on a special day
6. Native Americans = Indians

Yes or No? (page 35)

1. yes
2. no
3. no
4. yes
5. yes
6. yes
7. no
8. no
9. yes
10. no

Spelling (page 36)

A. 1. Am<u>e</u>rica
   2. Col<u>u</u>mb<u>u</u>s Day
   3. Engl<u>i</u>sh
   4. fir<u>s</u>t
   5. fre<u>e</u>dom
   6. hel<u>p</u>ed
   7. liv<u>e</u>
   8. Oct<u>o</u>ber
   9. Th<u>a</u>nks<u>g</u>iving

B. 1. Native Americans were the <u>first</u> people to live in America.
   2. Christopher Columbus came to <u>America</u> in 1492.
   3. <u>Columbus Day</u> is in October.
   4. The Pilgrims came to America for religious <u>freedom</u>.
   5. The Pilgrims celebrated the first <u>Thanksgiving</u>.
   6. Most of the new colonists spoke <u>English</u>.

Say the Answer (page 36)

1. for religious freedom

2. the Mayflower

3. Native Americans

4. Thanksgiving

Try the Test (page 39)

1. C

2. D

3. A

4. B

5. D

6. A

Writing Test (page 39)

6. Columbus Day is in October.

7. We live in America.

8. Thanksgiving is in November.

9. I can speak English.

10. I can read and write English.

3. The Revolutionary War

Match (page 54)

1. stripes

2. George Washington

3. Independence Day

4. Declaration of Independence

5. war

6. army

What Does It Mean? (page 55)

1. commander in chief = army leader

2. Revolutionary War = war between England and America

3. independent = not part of another country

4. "All men are created equal." = All people have the same rights.

5. basic belief = important idea

Yes or No? (page 55)

1. no

2. no

3. yes

4. yes

5. yes

6. no

7. yes

8. no

9. no

Spelling (page 56)

A. 1. birthday

2. country

3. father

4. February

5. Independence

6. July

7. president

8. stand

9. stripes

B. 1. The father of our country is George Washington.

2. Washington's birthday is in February.

3. The stripes on the flag stand for the 13 original states.

4. Independence Day is in July.

5. The flag has 13 stripes.

6. George Washington was the first U.S. president.

7. July 4, 1776, is the birthday of the United States.

Say the Answer (page 56)

1. colonies
2. Delaware, Pennsylvania, New Jersey, Georgia, Connecticut, Massachusetts, Maryland, South Carolina, New Hampshire, Virginia, New York, North Carolina, Rhode Island
3. George Washington
4. the 13 original states
5. Patrick Henry
6. Independence Day

Try the Test (page 59)

1. D
2. B
3. C
4. A
5. D
6. C

Writing Test (page 59)

11. George Washington is the father of our country.
12. The birthday of the U.S. is July 4.
13. George Washington was the first U.S. president.
14. Independence Day is in July.
15. The U.S. flag has 13 stripes.

4. The Civil War

Match (page 70)

1. South
2. Civil War
3. North
4. Abraham Lincoln
5. slaves
6. signed

What Does It Mean? (page 71)

1. separate = not together
2. save the Union = keep all the states together
3. free = not slaves
4. Emancipation Proclamation = a paper to free the slaves
5. agree = say "OK"
6. grow = get bigger

Yes or No? (page 71)

1. no
2. no
3. yes
4. yes
5. yes
6. yes
7. no
8. no
9. yes

Spelling (page 72)

A.
1. Abraham Lincoln
2. Civil War
3. free
4. grow
5. North
6. saved
7. South
8. work
9. Union
10. United States
11. won
12. paper

B. 1. During the <u>Civil War</u>, Lincoln was president.

2. A slave is a person who is not <u>free</u>.

3. People in the <u>South</u> wanted to keep their slaves.

4. Abraham Lincoln saved the <u>Union</u>.

5. The North <u>won</u> the Civil War.

6. <u>Abraham Lincoln</u> signed the Emancipation Proclamation.

7. The U.S. began to <u>grow</u> after the Revolutionary War.

Say the Answer (page 72)

1. Abraham Lincoln

2. freed slaves

3. Abraham Lincoln

Try the Test (page 75)

1. B

2. A

3. D

4. A

5. C

6. A

Writing Test (page 75)

16. The United States is a free country.

17. Abraham Lincoln saved the Union.

18. The North won the Civil War.

19. Presidents' Day is in February.

20. We live in North America.

5. Later History

Match (page 86)

1. immigrants

2. minorities

3. Alaska and Hawaii

4. Martin Luther King Jr.

5. United Nations

What Does It Mean? (page 87)

1. enemies = countries the U.S. fought against

2. purpose = reason

3. equal rights = the same rights for everybody

4. population = number of people

5. millions = more than 1,000,000

6. discuss = talk about

7. grew = got bigger

8. resolve = fix

Yes or No? (page 87)

1. yes

2. yes

3. no

4. yes

5. yes

6. no

7. no

8. yes

Spelling (page 88)

A. 1. Am<u>e</u>ricans

2. h<u>o</u>liday

3. hon<u>o</u>r

4. lea<u>d</u>er

5. <u>c</u>ame

6. Memo<u>r</u>ial Day

7. ta<u>l</u>k

8. righ<u>t</u>s

9. Ve<u>t</u>erans Day

B. 1. After the Civil War, many immigrants <u>came</u> to the U.S.

2. We <u>honor</u> Americans who fought in U.S. wars.

3. <u>Memorial Day</u> is in May.

4. Martin Luther King Jr. Day is a national <u>holiday</u>.

5. Dr. Martin Luther King Jr. was a <u>leader</u> in the Civil Rights movement.

6. All Americans have <u>rights</u>.

7. Countries <u>talk</u> together at the United Nations.

Say the Answer (page 88)

1. to keep peace in the world

2. Germany, Japan, and Italy

3. Alaska and Hawaii

4. a civil rights leader

Try the Test (page 91)

1. B
2. C
3. B
4. D
5. A
6. A

Writing Test (page 91)

21. Americans live in freedom.

22. All Americans have rights.

23. Memorial Day is in May.

24. Veterans Day is in November.

25. The United States has 50 states.

History Review

People to Remember (page 92)

1. Thomas Jefferson
2. the King of England
3. Martin Luther King Jr.
4. Abraham Lincoln
5. George Washington
6. Christopher Columbus

Groups to Remember (page 93)

1. the United Nations
2. Native Americans
3. immigrants
4. the Colonial Army
5. U.S. minorities
6. Pilgrims

When Did It Happen? (page 94)

1492 Columbus came to America.

1600s The first colonists from England came to America.

1776 The 13 colonies became the United States.

1860s The North and the South fought in the Civil War.

1940s The U.S. fought in World War II.

1959 Hawaii joined the Union.

1960s Martin Luther King Jr. helped minorities.

When Is the Holiday? (page 95)

1. Thanksgiving is in November.

2. Independence Day is in July.

3. Presidents' Day is in February.

4. Martin Luther King Jr. Day is in January.

5. Columbus Day is in October.

6. Memorial Day is in May.

History Test A (page 96)

1. B
2. A
3. D
4. A
5. B
6. A
7. B
8. A

Writing Test

A. There are 13 stripes on the flag.

B. The United States has 50 states.

History Test B (page 97)

1. C
2. A
3. D
4. B
5. A
6. B
7. D
8. A
9. D
10. C

Writing Test

A. There are 50 stars on the American flag.

B. I can read English.

6. The Constitution

Match (page 112)

1. freedom of speech
2. freedom of assembly
3. freedom of religion
4. freedom of the press
5. freedom of religion
6. freedom of the press

What Does It Mean? (page 113)

1. permission = The government says it's OK.
2. freedom of speech = You can say what you want.
3. the Bill of Rights = the first 10 amendments to the Constitution
4. the Constitution = the highest law of the U.S.
5. amendment = change to the Constitution
6. highest = number 1
7. branches = parts of the government

Yes or No? (page 113)

1. yes
2. yes
3. yes
4. no
5. no
6. yes
7. no
8. yes

Spelling (page 114)

A. 1. Bill of Rights

   2. citizens

3. Constitu<u>t</u>ion

4. giv<u>e</u>s

5. high<u>e</u>st

6. lan<u>d</u>

7. l<u>a</u>w

8. spe<u>e</u>ch

9. vo<u>t</u>e

B. 1. The <u>Constitution</u> is the supreme law.

2. The first 10 amendments are the <u>Bill of Rights.</u>

3. The Bill of Rights gives freedom of <u>speech</u> to Americans.

4. The highest law of the <u>land</u> is the Constitution.

5. Only U.S. citizens can <u>vote</u>.

6. All <u>citizens</u> have rights.

Say the Answer (page 114)

1. freedom of assembly, freedom of the press, freedom of speech, freedom of religion

2. vote, travel with a U.S. passport, bring close relatives to live in the U.S., work for the U.S. government

3. the right to vote

4. 1787

5. all people living in the U.S.

6. the Preamble

7. 14th, 15th, and 19th Amendments

Try the Test (page 117)

1. B

2. D

3. A

4. B

5. B

6. C

Writing Test (page 117)

26. The Constitution is the highest law of the land.

27. Americans have freedom of speech.

28. The Bill of Rights gives us freedom.

29. U.S. citizens can vote in elections.

30. Citizens have the right to vote.

7. The Executive Branch

What Does It Mean? (page 127)

1. advise = help

2. military = army, navy, air force, and marines

3. Cabinet = group of people who help the president

4. natural-born citizen = born in the U.S.

5. official = for the government

6. the White House = The president lives here.

7. inaugurated = officially becomes president

Yes or No? (page 127)

1. yes

2. no

3. no

4. yes

5. yes

6. no

7. yes

8. no

9. no

10. no

Spelling (page 128)

A.
1. ye<u>a</u>rs
2. <u>N</u>ovemb<u>e</u>r
3. ser<u>v</u>e
4. bo<u>r</u>n
5. vic<u>e</u> presi<u>d</u>ent
6. W<u>h</u>ite Ho<u>u</u>se

B.
1. A president can <u>serve</u> for two terms.
2. We elect a president for four <u>years</u>.
3. We elect a president in <u>November</u>.
4. The <u>White House</u> is the official home of the president.
5. The <u>vice president</u> becomes the new president if the president dies.
6. The president must be a natural-<u>born</u> citizen.

Say the Answer (page 128)

1. The answer will change with time.
2. the people
3. the president, the Cabinet, and departments under them
4. two
5. November
6. in Washington, D.C.
7. January
8. be 35 years old and a natural-born citizen

Try the Test (page 131)

1. B
2. B
3. D
4. C
5. D
6. A

Writing Test (page 131)

31. Election Day is in November.
32. The vice president helps the president.
33. A president can serve two terms.
34. The president serves for four years.
35. The president lives in the White House.

8. The Legislative Branch

What Does It Mean? (page 145)

1. Congress = the Senate and the House of Representatives
2. the Capitol = Congress meets here.
3. duty = job
4. meets = works together
5. the House of Representatives = group of 435 lawmakers
6. the Senate = group of 100 lawmakers

Yes or No? (page 145)

1. yes
2. yes
3. no
4. no
5. no
6. yes
7. no
8. yes
9. yes
10. no

Spelling (page 146)

A.
1. Capito<u>l</u>
2. Cong<u>r</u>ess
3. liv<u>e</u>

4. e<u>a</u>ch

5. m<u>a</u>kes

6. <u>tw</u>o

7. mee<u>t</u>s

8. peopl<u>e</u>

9. ho<u>u</u>se

10. sen<u>a</u>tors

11. Sena<u>t</u>e

B. 1. There are two senators for <u>each</u> state.

2. Representatives are elected by the <u>people</u>.

3. Congress <u>makes</u> the laws.

4. Congress <u>meets</u> in the <u>Capitol</u>.

5. There are two houses, or parts, of <u>Congress</u>.

6. States with many <u>people</u> have many representatives.

Say the Answer (page 146)

1. the Senate and the House of Representatives

2. the people

3. The answer depends on where you live.

4. the Speaker of the House

5. the president

6. the building where Congress meets

7. There is no limit.

8. There is no limit.

Try the Test (page 149)

1. B

2. C

3. A

4. B

5. C

6. D

Writing Test (page 149)

36. Each state has two senators.

37. Congress makes the laws.

38. Congress meets in the Capitol.

39. There are two houses of Congress.

40. Senators are elected by the people.

9. The Judicial Branch

What Does It Mean? (page 157)

1. the Supreme Court = the highest court in the U.S.

2. interprets = explains

3. Chief Justice = leader of the Supreme Court

4. constitutional = agrees with the Constitution

5. unconstitutional = doesn't agree with the Constitution

6. federal = for the whole U.S.

7. nominates = picks

Yes or No? (page 157)

1. yes

2. no

3. yes

4. no

5. no

6. yes

7. no

8. yes

9. yes

10. no

11. yes

Spelling (page 158)

A. 1. m<u>u</u>st

2. Supr<u>e</u>me Cour<u>t</u>

3. m<u>a</u>ny

4. W<u>a</u>shington, D.C.

5. w<u>o</u>rk

6. ni<u>n</u>e

B. 1. The highest U.S. court is the <u>Supreme Court</u>.

2. The <u>work</u> of the Supreme Court is to interpret laws.

3. The Supreme Court meets in <u>Washington</u>, <u>D.C.</u>

4. A law that is unconstitutional <u>must</u> be changed.

5. There are <u>nine</u> justices on the Supreme Court.

Say the Answer (page 158)

1. The answer will change with time.

2. the Supreme Court and other federal courts

3. the president

4. to interpret laws

5. nine

Try the Test (page 161)

1. A

2. C

3. B

4. D

5. A

6. B

Writing Test (page 161)

41. The Supreme Court is in Washington, D.C.

42. Washington, D.C., is the U.S. capital.

43. We must honor our country's flag.

44. The White House is in Washington, D.C.

45. I want to be an American citizen.

Government Review

Match (page 162)

1. the Capitol

2. Congress

3. the U.S. military

4. the Supreme Court

5. a justice

6. the White House

Which Branch Are They In? (page 163)

Executive: president, vice president, Cabinet

Legislative: senators, representatives

Judicial: justices

Important Numbers (page 164)

1. 9

2. 4

3. 13

4. 27

5. 100

6. 6

7. 435

8. 50

9. 10

10. 2

11. 13

12. 2

Which Branch Is It? (page 165)

1. J

2. L

3. J

4. L

5. E

6. J

7. L

8. L

9. J

10. E

11. L

12. L

13. J

14. E

Which Is It? (page 166)

1. D

2. E

3. B

4. D

5. E

6. E

7. C

8. C

9. D

10. B

11. D

Government Test A (page 167)

1. A

2. D

3. C

4. D

5. C

6. A

7. A

8. D

Writing Test

A. I want to be a U.S. citizen.

B. Congress is elected by the people.

Government Test B (page 168)

1. A

2. D

3. A

4. C

5. A

6. C

7. B

8. C

9. B

10. A

Writing Test

A. The president is our leader.

B. The Constitution is the highest law.

Review Test 1 (pages 172–173)

1. B

2. C

3. B

4. D

5. A
6. C
7. A
8. C
9. C
10. D
11. B
12. C
13. A
14. B
15. C
16. C
17. B
18. B
19. A
20. B

Writing Test

A. The Statue of Liberty stands for freedom.

B. The Supreme Court is the highest U.S. court.

Review Test 2 (pages 174–175)

1. D
2. A
3. C
4. B
5. D
6. C
7. A
8. B
9. A
10. C
11. C

12. C
13. D
14. B
15. D
16. D
17. A
18. A
19. B
20. D

Writing Test

A. Independence Day is the birthday of the United States.

B. Only U.S. citizens can vote.